THE SOUTH CHINA SEA DISPUTES AND THE U.S.–CHINA CONTEST

International Law and Geopolitics

Series on Contemporary China

(ISSN: 1793-0847)

This series will include books on state-of-the-art developments in computational and experimental methods in structures, and as such it will comprise several volumes covering the latest developments. Each volume will consist of single-authored work or several chapters written by the leading researchers in the field. The aim will be to provide the fundamental concepts of experimental and computational methods as well as their relevance to real world problems.

The scope of the series covers the entire spectrum of structures in engineering. As such it will cover both classical topics in mechanics, as well as emerging scientific and engineering disciplines, such as: smart structures, nanoscience and nanotechnology; NEMS and MEMS; micro- and nano-device modelling; functional and smart material systems.

*Published**

Vol. 43 *The South China Sea Disputes and the U.S.–China Contest International Law and Geopolitics*
by James C Hsiung

Vol. 42 *The South China Sea Disputes: Historical, Geopolitical and Legal Studies*
edited by Tsu-Sung Hsieh

Vol. 41 *Moralization of China*
by Xin Liu

Vol. 40 *Social Construction in Contemporary China*
edited by Xueyi Lu

Vol. 39 *China's Economic Statecraft: Co-optation, Cooperation, and Coercion*
edited by Mingjiang Li

Vol. 38 *The Domestic Dynamics of China's Energy Diplomacy*
by Chi Zhang

Vol. 37 *Understanding Chinese Society: Changes and Transformations*
by Eileen Yuk-ha Tsang

Vol. 36 *Health Policy Reform in China: A Comparative Perspective*
by Jiwei Qian & Åke Blomqvist

Vol. 35 *Township Governance and Institutionalization in China*
by Shukai Zhao

*To view the complete list of the published volumes in the series, please visit:
http://www.worldscientific.com/series/scc

Series on Contemporary China – Vol. 43

THE SOUTH CHINA SEA DISPUTES AND THE U.S.–CHINA CONTEST

International Law and Geopolitics

James C Hsiung

New York University, USA

NEW JERSEY • LONDON • SINGAPORE • BEIJING • SHANGHAI • HONG KONG • TAIPEI • CHENNAI • TOKYO

Published by

World Scientific Publishing Co. Pte. Ltd.
5 Toh Tuck Link, Singapore 596224
USA office: 27 Warren Street, Suite 401-402, Hackensack, NJ 07601
UK office: 57 Shelton Street, Covent Garden, London WC2H 9HE

Library of Congress Cataloging-in-Publication Data
Names: Hsiung, James C., author.
Title: The South China Sea disputes and the U.S.–China contest: international law and geopolitics / James C. Hsiung.
Description: New Jersey : World Scientific, [2018] |
Series: Series on contemporary China ; ISSN 1793-0847.
Identifiers: LCCN 2017040693 | ISBN 9789813231092
Subjects: LCSH: China--Foreign relations--Southeast Asia. |
United States--Foreign relations--China. | South China Sea--International status.
Classification: LCC DS525.9.C5 H75 2018 | DDC 327.73051--dc23
LC record available at https://lccn.loc.gov/2017040693

British Library Cataloguing-in-Publication Data
A catalogue record for this book is available from the British Library.

For any available supplementary material, please visit
http://www.worldscientific.com/worldscibooks/10.1142/10738#t=suppl

Desk Editor: Dong Lixi

Typeset by Stallion Press
Email: enquiries@stallionpress.com

Printed in Singapore

About the Author

Dr James C Hsiung (PhD, Columbia Univ.) is Professor of Politics & International Law at New York University, where he teaches international politics, international law, and international governance.

His teaching and research interests extend to East Asian politics (China and Japan), Asian international relations, and Asian political cultures. Among his broad professional concerns are the future of Asia Pacific and America's strategic stakes in Asia. He is author and editor of 24 books in English alone, including his *Twenty-First Century World Order and the Asia Pacific* (2001); *Anarchy and Order: The Interplay of Politics and Law in International Relations* (1997); *Asia Pacific in the New World Politics* (1993); *Comprehensive Security: Challenge for Pacific Asia* (2004); *China and Japan at Odds: Deciphering the Perpetual Conflict* (2007); and *China into Its Second Rise: Myths, Puzzles, Paradoxes, and Challenge to Theory* (2012). His penultimate book is: *An Anatomy of Sino-Japanese Disputes & US Involvement: History and International Law* (May 2015). He is chief editor of *The Xi Jinping Era: His Comprehensive Strategy Toward the China Dream*, which appeared in August 2015.

Contents

Table of Acronyms (Common Abbreviations)

ADB	Asian Development Bank
AIIB	Asian Infrastructure Investment Bank
AJIL	*American Journal of International Law*
ASEAN	Association of Southeast Asian Nations
BPO	Business process outsourcing
BRI	Belt and Road Initiative (short for OBOR)
BRICS	The grouping of five emerging economies Brazil, Russia, India, China, and South Africa
CLCS	Commission on the Limits of the Continental Shelf
CPSU	Communist Party of the Soviet Union
CSIS	Center for Strategic and International Studies
DRVN	Democratic Republic of Vietnam (=North Vietnam, 1945–1975)
EEZ	Exclusive economic zone
HWA	Historic-waters approach
ICJ	International Court of Justice

IFA	Island-focused approach
IMF	International Monetary Fund
INF	Intermediate Nuclear Force treaty
IPE	International political economy (a new IR subfield)
IR	International relations (as a field of study)
ITLOS	International Tribunal for the Law of the Sea
MOI	Ministry of Internal Affairs
NDB	New Development Bank, under BRICS
NPC	National People's Congress
OBOR	One Belt One Road
PCA	Permanent Court of Arbitration
PCIJ	Permanent Court of International Justice
PRC	People's Republic of China
ROC	Republic of China
ROV	Republic of Vietnam (=South Vietnam, 1954–1975)
SCS	South China Sea
SRV	Socialist Republic of Vietnam (unified Vietnam, after 1975)
UNCLOS III	United Nations Convention on the Law of the Sea (1982)
UN ILC	U. N. International Law Commission
WWII	World War II

Table of Cases Cited

Case Concerning the Continental Shelf (Tunisia v. Libya, 1982), 1982 PCJ Reports.

Fisheries case (U.K. v. Norway) (1951), 1951 ICJ Reports, 116ff.

Fisheries Jurisdiction cases (Spain v. Canada), 1998 ICJ Reports 432; (U.K. v. Iceland) 1974 ICJ Reports 3.

Frontier Dispute case (Burkin Faso v. Republic of Mali), 1986 ICJ Reports 554.

Gulf of Maine case (U.S. v. Canada), 1984 ICJ Reports 300.

Island of Palmas case (U.S. v. The Netherlands, 1928), PCA, 1928, in 2 U.N Reports on Arbitral Awards, 829ff.

Land and Maritime Boundary (Cameroon v. Nigeria), 2002 ICJ Reports 94.

Legal Status of Eastern Greenland (Denmark v. Norway, 1933), 1933 P.C.I.J. (Series A/B), No. 53, at 71ff.

Ligitan and Sipadan Islands (Malaysia v. Indonesia), 2002 ICJ Reports 36.

North Atlantic Fisheries Arbitration (Great Britain v. U.S.), PCA Case No. 1909–01.

Pedra Branca, Middle Rocks, and South Ledge (Singapore v. Malaysia), ICJ Report 2008, at 12ff.

Philippines and China Arbitration. PCA Case No. 2013–19.

Introduction

The South China Sea (SCS) region has become a dragnet of international conflicts, on a scale often compared to the disaster-prone Middle East. In a way, its tensions may be more treacherous, as they also embroil two giant powers in an intricate contest: the United States, the extant superpower, and China, the emergent superpower.

To begin with, the tensions were endemic to the region with long-standing disputes due to the overlapping claims to parts of the SCS advanced by its surrounding neighboring states. The competing claimants include China (both the mainland and Taiwan), Vietnam, the Philippines, Malaysia, and Brunei. Regional competition intensified after 1968 following reports that flaunted vital natural resources (oil and natural gas) under the SCS seabed, as noted in Chapter 1.

Of late, the conflict-ridden milieu became more acute and sinister, as the U.S.–China contest deteriorated. Though it laid no claim to any part of the SCS, the United States was alarmed by the rise of China, and hence the attendant "China threat" scare trumpeted by many neorealist International Relations (IR) analysts and media gurus alike.

The SCS imbroglio, in fact, entailed two separate tangles: (a) a legal tangle bedeviling China's relations with its Asian competing claimant neighbors, whose respective positions are compared and analyzed in Chapter 2, and (b) a geopolitical tangle at the heart of the U.S.–China contest. For the Chinese, the two tangles are interrelated in that, for instance, the legal assault by the Philippines by filing a complaint against China in 2013 to a Permanent Court of Arbitration (PCA) Tribunal was egged on by Washington, which provided expert legal assistance. And, its own refusal to participate in the arbitration followed by its rejection of the Tribunal's final award brought upon itself a scofflaw stigma that only resulted in China's further isolation. This in turn made the U.S. naval surveillance in the SCS, right under China's nose, sound more "justified" under the pretext of protecting the freedom of navigation.

China's nonparticipation, as we try to show in Chapter 4, turned out to be a blessing for the Philippines, which had an opportune chance to both pick the arbitrators and to name the law to be applied by the Tribunal. Thus, the 1982 U.N. Convention on the Law of the Sea (UNCLOS III), preferred by the Philippines, became the exclusive source of law against which China's claim, based as it is on the concept of "historic waters," was to be evaluated. Thus, China's loss was a foregone conclusion, because the UNCLOS III is totally silent on the issue of "historic waters," which, nevertheless, finds firm support in general international law (as opposed to treaty law), as Chapter 3 tries to show.

An injunction in the preambular part of UNCLOS III declares: "matters not regulated by this Convention continue to be governed by the rules and principles of general international law." The arbitral tribunal, however, totally disregarded the injunction. Parenthetically, this opens up a potential avenue by which China may be able to vindicate its own rights and exonerate itself from the undeserved scofflaw stigma, as we ascertain how this can be done in the concluding chapter.

As it was suggested in some quarters[1], the U.S. attention to the SCS region was drawn out of a perceived injustice in which an Asian ally (the Philippines) and an emerging partner (Vietnam, after 1975), among others, were being "bullied" by the more powerful and "assertive" Chinese claimant. However, I would like to see whether it might also be true that the United States was drawn by its geopolitical instincts to the imperative of combating the alleged China threat. As such, the SCS just became a convenient stage on which the U.S. geopolitical contest with China unfolded as a consequence.

Punctuating the gravity of the great power contest, rumors of a war, possibly imminent, between China and the United States took off in the days immediately after the election of Donald Trump as the U.S. President in late 2016. Scholarly speculations zeroed in on a war snare known as the Thucydides Trap, named after the ancient Greek historian who studied and pontificated on the Peloponnesian war as resulting from Athens's rise and the fear that it instilled in Sparta. We devoted, not one but two chapters (Chapters 6 and 7) to an in-depth examination of how true the rumored war between the United States and China would come about in reality. Contrary to the habitual disregard of history in most media reports, these two chapters go through the long historical background of Sino–U.S. relations, beginning from the 19th century and continuing on through the ups and downs in between until their normalization after 1979, only to be marred by the "China threat" scare stemming from China's relentless rise after the turn of the new century. Chapter 6 tries to see if the past sheds any light on the current clash of visions, based on mutual (mis-) perceptions and the chain of escalatory reactions between the two sides that seem to characterize the spirals in the on-going U.S.–China contest.

In Chapter 7, we turn to the differing strategies adopted by the two sides. The U.S. strategy is conceived in militarization, in fact naval militarization in the Asia Pacific, in particular, the SCS, as

[1] Firestein, David. "The U.S.–China Perception Gap in the South China Sea," *The Diplomat*, August 9, 2016.

codified in Public Law 113–291. By contrast, the Chinese, under Xi Jinping, have deliberately opted for a geo-economics-oriented strategy, for the sake of pursuing a "nonsymmetric competition" with the United States. The ultimate purpose is to veer off from a military confrontation and, moreover, to avoid getting trapped into a race for the control of regional and global public order. The end result from this choice of a divergent strategy as such is that a violent end to the bilateral contest with the United States is, happily, not in the cards.

The final chapter (Chapter 8), which is to ascertain a possible way out of the geopolitical and legal tangles, has two parts, the first of which deals with the veracity of the "China threat" scare. We trace the unfolding waves of discernible shifts in the intellectual climate surrounding the China debate, until finally the earlier scare lost its punch, both because of a growing consensus on China's relative power deficit and its lack of an identifiable "intention" to try to dominate and replace the United States as the ultimate hegemonic power. The second part of the final chapter addresses the question of how China might try to rid itself of the scofflaw stigma, the removal of which is absolutely necessary if China is ever to appear as a credible power with the moral "authority" (in the sense as David Lake used it)[2] to work hand in hand with the United States, conceivably in a condominium, for the maintenance of peace and stability in regional and global public order. Peace can come only then, but not before it. And, China can cleanse its name by removing its undeserved scofflaw stigma only if it takes the adjudicative steps, as we suggest in the final chapter, but not without.

The book begins with concerns about regional tensions surrounding the SCS that began with the overlapping claims by competing Asian neighbors, but culminated in a U.S.–China contest, sustained by America's geopolitical instincts to the rise of an unstoppable China, and to the "China threat" scare that came with it. The final part of the book returns to our enduring interests in finding a way out of the legal and

[2] Lake, David. 2003. "The New Sovereignty in International Relations," *International Studies Review*, vol. 4, no. 5: 303–323.

geopolitical tangles associated with the SCS, after discussing the unsustainable scare about the China threat and the lack of an empirically identifiable Chinese intent to dominate and replace America as the leader over regional and global public order.

Chapter

1

The Provenance and Ramifications of the SCS Conflicts: Law, Resources, and Geopolitics

The South China Sea (SCS) may, by common sense, be assumed to be part of the Pacific Ocean. But, in this book, we treat it as a separate body of waters in its own right, due to its distinctive status arising from a combination of four peculiar factors: (a) its vital importance as a hubbub of trade, since one-third of the world's shipping (valued at $5.3 trillion in 2015) sails through its waters; (b) its abundant resources, including oil and natural gas; (c) the wide attention it commands because of the clashes arising from the neighboring nations' overlapping sovereign claims; and (d) post-2010 U.S. geopolitical interests in the region as a strategic site of rivalry with the rerising China, although largely dressed as a freedom of navigation dispute.

For amplification of (a) above, let me add that the oil transported through the Malacca Strait through the Indian Ocean en route to

East Asia via the SCS is triple the amount that passes through the Suez Canal, and 14 times that through the Panama Canal.[1]

This body of waters, stretching over 1.4 million square miles, has been the locale for activities of, or interactions between, the surrounding societies going back to prehistorical times, through the Western colonial dominance in the region (dating from the 16th to the mid-20th century), down to the post–Cold War era. Unlike in the East China Sea disputes, through much of this long stretch of time the SCS, surprisingly, had its share of relative peaceful tranquility. Exceptions were found in the past strife associated with the intrusion of Western colonialism and, more notably, the truculent inroads by the Japanese Imperial Army (1930s to 1945).[2] Even the assertion by the parties of their competing claims, in the past, was relatively muted, by comparison. But, in more recent years, this maritime scene has become a tinderbox of explosive international tensions of rising magnitude, largely for two reasons, namely: (a) the salience of the newly identified abundance in oil deposits among other resources in SCS and (b) the spillover of the United States' Asia Pivot policy. The following discussion will tackle each of these points separately, in greater depth.

Highlight on SCS Resources: Competing Claims

A 1968 U.N. report revealed the discovery of rich oil and natural gas deposits in the SCS, according to one source.[3] This was echoed by a tweet on a Chinese blog, calling the SCS the "second Persian Sea" in reference to its vast oil deposits.[4] The Council on Foreign Relations

---

[1] Robert D. Kaplan, "Why the South China Sea Is So Crucial," http://www.businessinsider.com.a/.

[2] Cf. Bill Hayton, *The South China Sea: The Struggle for Power in Asia* (New Haven: Yale University Press, 2014), pp. 1–120; and the sources cited therein.

[3] "Zhongguo zhuzhang nanhai zhuquan di lishi yu fali yiju [The Historical and Legal Bases of China's Sovereign Claim to the South China Sea]," *zhongguoguoqingzhongguonet*, April 11, 2014; retrieved February 1, 2016.

[4] "Nanhai guofang jingji yiyi jie zhongyao yucheng dier posiwan [The Defense and Economic Significance of South China Sea Made It a Second Persian Gulf]," news on the *Tengxun Blog*; retrieved October 1, 2015, online.

in New York gave a more modest, but still staggering, estimate: some 11 billion barrels of oil and 190 trillion cubic feet of natural gas deposits under the subsoil of the SCS.[5]

It may not be coincidental that the conflicts with China by some Southeast Asian contending neighbors, such as Vietnam and the Philippines, began to hike in the years immediately following 1968. For instance, the struggle over the Paracels between Vietnam and China began in 1970; and a war broke out in 1974, in which Vietnam was defeated, and China took back the complete control of the island group. On its part, the Philippines in 1971 announced its claim to islands in the Spratlys adjacent to its territory, which it renamed Kalayaan and incorporated into Palawan Province the following year.[6] On March 11, 1976, the first Philippine oil company "discovered" an oilfield off Palawan island. Also in the 1970s, the Philippines, Malaysia, and other countries began referring to the Spratly islands as included in their own territory. President Ferdinand Marcos of the Philippines, for example, issued Presidential decree No. 1596, on June 11, 1978, declaring the Spratlys (referred to as the Kalayaan Island Group) as Philippine territory.[7]

To bring things up to date, the search for oil even brought India and Japan to the SCS, by means of cooperative deals signed with Vietnam in the early 21st century. On July 22, 2011, an Indian amphibious assault vessel, the INS Airavat, on a friendly visit to Vietnam, was contacted, some 45 nautical miles off the Vietnamese coast, by the Chinese navy that it was entering Chinese waters.[8] In reply, the Indian side quipped that seeing no ship or aircraft in view, the INS Airavat just proceeded on her onward journey as scheduled. Citing freedom of navigation, it continued that the Indian vessel

---

[5] See "China's Maritime Disputes," a Council on Foreign Relations presentation (January 2017).

[6] Cf. Timeline of Events in "Territorial Disputes in the South China Sea," from Wikipedia, the free encyclopedia, retrieved February 26, 2017, online.

[7] "Presidential Decree No. 1596 — Declaring Certain Area Part of the Philippine Territory and Providing for Their Government and Administration." *Chan Robles Law Library*, June 11, 1978.

[8] "China Face-Off in South China Sea," *DNA India Report*, July 22, 2011.

meant no harm or confrontation.[9] In September 2011, shortly after Vietnam and China had signed an agreement seeking to contain a dispute over the SCS,[10] India announced that ONGC Videsh Ltd, an Indian overseas investment company, had signed a three-year agreement with PetroVietnam for developing long-term cooperation in the oil sector. The announcement also said that India had accepted Vietnam's offer of exploration in certain specified blocks in the SCS.[11]

Vietnam and Japan, early in 1978, also reached an agreement on the development of oil in the SCS. By 2012, Vietnam had concluded some 60 oil and gas exploration and production contracts with various foreign companies.[12] There are reports that show that Vietnam, which used to be an oil-poor country, had an average production of 298 barrels of crude a day (298 BBL/D), during 1994–2016, making it an oil exporting country.[13]

As if not to be left behind, China's first independently designed and constructed oil drilling platform in SCS, *Ocean Oil 981* (海洋石油 981), also began its first drilling operation in 2012. The platform is located 320 km (c. 200 miles) southeast of Hong Kong.[14]

China's Connections: An Inherent Link to a Historic Waters Claim

After waiting out a period of hesitancy in the face of the Vietnamese and Philippine challenges, noted earlier, China's National People's Congress (NPC) passed a "Law on Territorial Waters and Adjacent Regions" in 1992. The Law formalized the People's Republic's 1958 "Proclamation on the Territorial Sea." I wish to stress that for a true

---

[9] South China Analysis Group whitepaper, September 2, 2011.

[10] Vietnam-PRC Gulf of Tonkin Agreement, 2,000.

[11] "China Paper Warns India Off Vietnam Oil Deal," *Reuters Article*, October 16, 2011.

[12] Leszek Buszynski, "The South China Sea: Oil, Maritime Claims, and U.S.–China Strategic Rivalry," *The Washington Quarterly*, Spring 2012.

[13] "Vietnam Crude Oil Production, 1994–2016," www.tgradingeconomics.com/vietnam/crude-oil-production; retrieved March 4, 2017, online.

[14] "南海钻井平台工人直升机上下班 [Workers Taking Helicopters to Go to Work and Back at the SCS Oil Platform]," *NetEase News*, May 11, 2012.

understanding of their legal and practical significance, these two documents must be read in the light of a map made by the Chinese in 1947, two years after the end of World War II (WWII), from which China under the Chiang Kai-shek government emerged as a victor power, on the side of the Western WWII Allies.

While China's claim to the SCS goes back to the pre-Christian era (more details in Chapter 2), the Japanese Imperial Army during WWII occupied the major island groups, including Paracels and Spratlys. Under the Cairo Declaration (November 1943) and the Potsdam Declaration (July 1945), however, the WWII Allies agreed on a demand for the soon-to-be-defeated Japan that it must surrender (and return) all territories it had pilfered ("stolen") from their original owners. Hence, after the war, the Republic of China (ROC), under Chiang Kai-shek, recovered these islands from the Japanese in 1946, with the logistical (naval) support from its U.S. ally.[15] After regaining control of the SCS, the ROC government in 1947 drew an 11-dash line map delineating the maritime extent of Chinese control of the waters (including the islands) of the SCS. The map was known as "Map of South China Sea Islands."[16] It followed a much earlier "Map of Chinese Islands in South China Sea" (*Zhongguo nanhai daoyu tu*), published by the ROC's Land and Water Maps Inspection Committee in 1935.[17] The 1947 map showed the extent of China's historic title over most of the maritime region in the SCS, and in international law it would come under the concept of "historic waters" (see discussion in Chapters 2 and 3). See the following map:

It should be noted that this map, showing the Chinese U-shaped line, resembling a cow's tongue, indicates that China does not claim the entire SCS, as alleged by almost every critic and accuser of China's

[15] A fact explicitly acknowledged by PRC's foreign minister, Wang Yi, at a press conference jointly staged with his Australian counterpart, in Canberra, February 7, 2017, as reported in *Qiao Bao* (New York: The China Press, February 8, 2017), p. 4.

[16] Peter J. Brown, "Calculated Ambiguity in the South China Sea," *Asia Times*, December 8, 2009; retrieved February 5, 2014, online.

[17] Cf. "Limits in the Seas" (PDF), Office of Ocean and Polar Affairs, U.S. State Department.

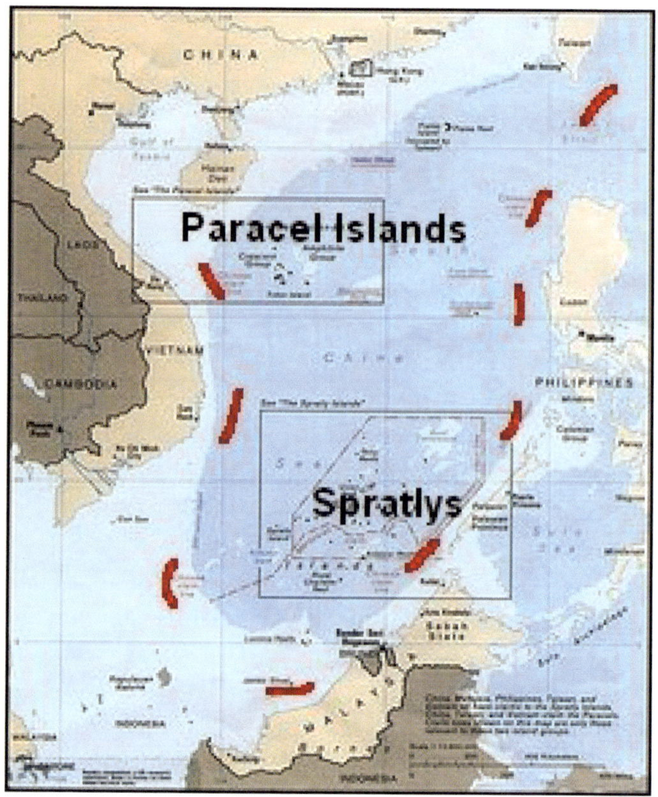

Figure 1.1 (Internet Photo)

"assertive" claim. The space in between the U-shaped broken line and the putative coastlines of the surrounding states, such as today's Vietnam, Malaysia, Brunei, and the Philippines, clearly manifests an allowance for the territorial seas that they may opt to claim (after they emerged from colonial rule).

Apparently, this relative self-restraint may have been a reason why the map did not draw any international objection at the time. Another reason was that "historic waters" was a concept accepted by the prevailing international law at the time.

It is noteworthy that the Chinese map was immediately adopted in the 1947 edition of the Rand McNally Map of China, as shown in Figure 1.2, suggesting instant international recognition.

1947 Rand McNally map lists Paracels as Chinese

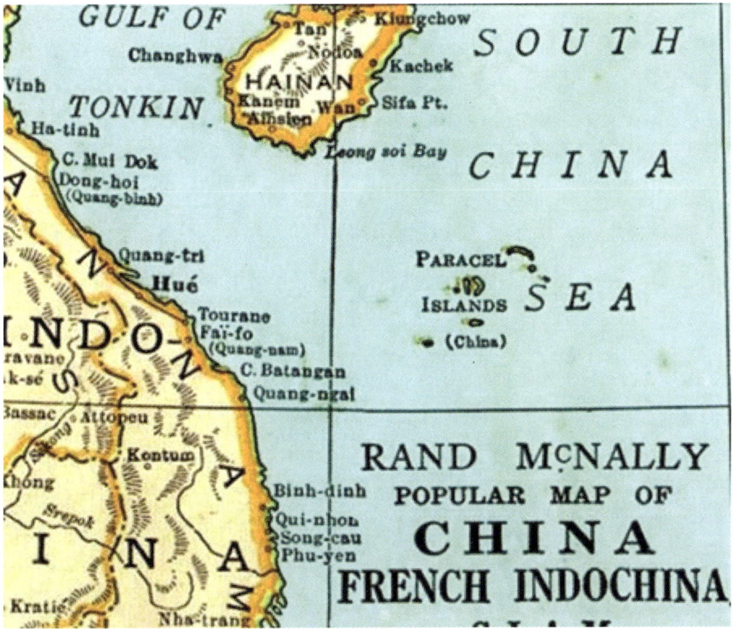

Figure 1.2 "China" is Shown Underneath the Paracel Islands in Parenthesis on the Map Made by Rand McNally in 1947. (Internet Photo)

After the Communists took power in China in 1949, the new People's Republic of China (PRC) government adopted the 11-dash line but reduced it to nine, eliminating the two dashes most adjacent to the Gulf of Tonkin as a gesture of friendship toward Ho Chi Minh's Vietnam. After evacuating to Taiwan after losing the civil war on the mainland, the ROC government (now resettled in Taiwan), nevertheless, continues its claim to the SCS as before, but used the coopted name of the 9-dash line (rather than the original 11-dash line), in support of its claim.[18]

As mentioned earlier, the Government in Beijing, on September 4, 1958, issued the Proclamation regarding the breath of China's

[18] "Taiwan Sticks to Its Guns, to U.S. Chagrin," *Asia Times* (1999); STRATFOR's Global Intelligence Update (July 14, 1999); retrieved May 1, 2014, online.

territorial sea, which extended 12 nautical miles seaward from the China coast. It stated that the rule applied to "all Chinese territories, including ... the Dongsha islands [Pratas], the Xisha Islands [Paracels], the Zhongsha Islands [Macclesfield Bank], the Nansha Islands [Spratlys] ..." (emphasis added). Ten days later, in an official note to Chinese Premier Zhou Enlai, the Vietnamese Prime Minister, Pham Van Dong, declared "the Government of the Democratic Republic of Vietnam recognizes and supports the declaration of the Government of the People's Republic of China's territorial sea made on September 4, 1958." (Pham Van Dong's letter written in Vietnamese, reproduced below.[19])

Special attention should be paid to this 1958 documentary evidence, attesting to the official Vietnamese government's explicit recognition that the "Chinese territories" included the Paracels, which is now claimed by Vietnam in competition. The obvious reason is a hidden struggle for the oil resources near the Paracel island group. The conflict surfaced in early 2014 when the Chinese moved its Ocean Oil 981 oil rig to the territorial waters of the Paracel island group, which even by the Vietnamese Premier Pham Van Dong document should be within China's territory. In its wake, however, Vietnamese anti-Chinese protests boiled over, from mob rioting, ransacking, to torching of Chinese (and other Asian but mistaken to be Chinese) factories and companies in different parts of Vietnam. Among rampant reactions worldwide, the U.S. State Department sided with the Vietnamese and blamed the violence and carnage on Chinese "unilateral action [that] appears to be part of a broader pattern of Chinese behavior to advance its claim over disputed territory in a manner that undermines peace and stability in the region."[20]

---

[19] Taken from Frank Ching, "Paracels Islands Dispute," *Far Eastern Economic Review* (Hong Kong), February 10, 1994, which reproduced the original Pham Va Dong letter written in Vietnamese.

[20] "Vietnamese Mobs Torch Foreign Factories in Anti-Chinese Protests," *Los Angeles Times*, May 14, 2014, online.

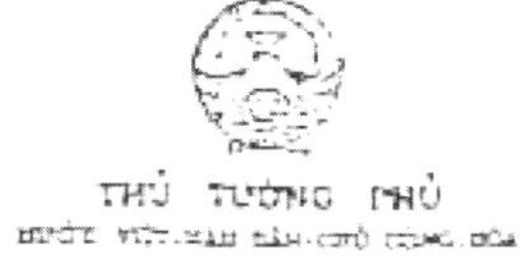
THỦ TƯỚNG PHỦ
NƯỚC VIỆT-NAM DÂN-CHỦ CỘNG-HÒA

Thưa Đồng chí Tổng lý,

Chúng tôi xin trân trọng báo tin để Đồng chí Tổng lý rõ:

Chính phủ nước Việt-nam Dân chủ Cộng hoà ghi nhận và tán thành bản tuyên bố, ngày 4 tháng 9 năm 1958, của Chính phủ nước Cộng hoà Nhân dân Trung-hoa, quyết định về hải phận của Trung-quốc.

Chính phủ nước Việt-nam Dân chủ Cộng hoà tôn trọng quyết định ấy và sẽ chỉ thị cho các cơ quan Nhà nước có trách nhiệm triệt để tôn trọng hải phận 12 hải lý của Trung-quốc, trong mọi quan hệ với nước Cộng hoà Nhân dân Trung hoa trên mặt bể.

Chúng tôi xin kính gửi Đồng chí Tổng lý lời chào rất trân trọng./.

Hà-nội, ngày 14 tháng 9 năm 1958

PHẠM VĂN ĐỒNG
Thủ tướng Chính phủ
Nước Việt-nam Dân chủ Cộng hoà

Kính gửi:
Đồng chí CHU ÂN LAI
Tổng lý Quốc vụ viện
Nước Cộng hoà Nhân dân Trung-hoa
tại
BẮC-KINH.

Nguyên bản Công-hàm của Phạm Văn Đồng xác-nhận hải-phận lãnh-thổ 12 hải-lý, gửi Chu Ân Lai ngày 14 tháng 9 năm 1958

VIỆT-NAM TẬP-CHÍ 42

THỦ TƯỚNG PHỦ
NƯỚC VIỆT NAM DÂN CHỦ CỘNG HÒA

Thưa Đồng chí Tổng lý,

Chúng tôi xin trân trọng báo tin để Đồng chí Tổng lý rõ:

Chính phủ nước Việt-nam Dân chủ Cộng hòa ghi nhận và tán thành bản tuyên bố ngày 4 tháng 9 năm 1958, của Chính phủ nước Cộng hòa Nhân dân Trung-hoa, quyết định về hải phận của Trung Quốc.

Chính phủ nước Việt Nam Dân chủ Cộng hòa tôn trọng quyết định ấy và sẽ chỉ thị cho các cơ quan Nhà nước có trách nhiệm triệt để tôn trọng hải phận 12 hải lý của Trung-quốc, trong mọi quan hệ với nước Cộng hòa Nhân dân Trung hoa trên mặt bể.

Chúng tôi xin kính gởi Đồng chí Tổng lý lời chào rất trân trọng./.

Hà-nội, ngày 14 tháng 9 năm 1958

Phạm Văn Đồng

Thủ tướng Chính phủ
Nước Việt-nam Dân chủ Cộng Hòa

Figure 1.3

U.S. Support Stiffening the Backbone of China's Competitors

The other reason why the SCS conflicts spiked after 2010 was related to the United States' "Asia Pivot" policy of the Obama administration, which was cryptically explained as a "rebalancing" policy in Pacific Asia. As the official chiefly responsible for its implementation, Secretary of State Hillary Rodham Clinton demonstrated that it was, in reality, a policy of rallying Asian support in a not so subtle attempt to isolate and contain the (re-)rising China. An opportunity came handy when she attended the regional forum of the Association of Southeast Asian Nations (ASEAN) held in Hanoi, in July 2010. In her address at the forum, Secretary Clinton stressed that the United States, while remaining "neutral" in the disputes over territorial claims, had an "interest in freedom of navigation, open access to Asia's maritime commons, and respect for international law in the South China Sea." As the *New York Times* pointed out, her stance, although presented as an offer to help ease tensions, "amounts to a sharp rebuke to China."[21]

Later, my comments on Secretary Clinton's remarks will surface. But, first, let us not neglect the emboldening effects that her address enunciating America' stance had on China's neighbors, as can be seen in their subsequent harsh behavior vis-à-vis China. First, in both 2011 and 2012, the Philippines and China were locked in separate face-offs involving either fishing vessels or warships.[22] In one instance, in April 2012, the Philippine warship Gregorio del Pilar was involved in a standoff with two Chinese surveillance vessels in the Scarborough Shoal, an area claimed by both countries.[23] What gave additional encouragement to the Philippines was its annual joint naval exercise with the United States, which took place on April 14, 2012, in Palawan, Philippines. Moreover, with U.S. backup and legal assistance, the Philippines took its fight to the Permanent Court of Arbitration (PCA) in the Hague, in 2013, when it filed an application for arbitration in its territorial dispute with China in the SCS (discussed in Chapter 4).

Similar clashes also flared up between Vietnam and China. One such clash took place on May 26, 2011, scarcely 10 months after Secretary Clinton gave her pep talk to members of the ASEAN. It involved a confrontation between the Vietnamese *Binh Minh* 02 oil

---

[21] Mark Landler, "Offering to Aid Talks, U.S. Challenge China on Disputed Islands," *New York Times*, July 23, 2010, online.

[22] Tessa Jamandre, "China Fired at Filipino Fishermen in Jackson Atoll," *ABS-CBN News*, June 3, 2011; Bill Gertz. "Inside the Ring: China warship grounded," *Washington Times*, August 8, 2012.

[23] "China, Philippines Locked in Naval Standoff," *CNN*, April 11, 2012.

and gas survey ship and three Chinese maritime patrol vessels, some 80 miles off the south-central coast of Vietnam. The Vietnamese said the Chinese boats deliberately cut the survey ship's cables, but the Chinese denied the allegation.[24] The event stirred up unprecedented anti-China protests in Hanoi and Ho Chi Minh City, regardless.[25]

In all fairness, another no less potent contributing factor unrelated to U.S. instigation was a happenstance accruing from the May 13, 2009, deadline by which states parties to the 1982 U.N. Convention on the Law of the Sea (UNCLOS III) had to make seabed hydrocarbon claims under the Convention. It may have caused dormant island claims to surface and become inflamed, leading to the intensification of the SCS disputes and associated tensions between China and its competing claimants.[26] The United States, which is not a claimant, simply weighed in, as Secretary Hillary Clinton exemplified, to exploit the opportunity for rallying Asian support to help fulfill its geopolitical goal of balancing against China.

An Evaluation of Hillary Clinton's Two Charges Against China

Two remarks stood out from Secretary Clinton's address at the ASEAN forum, noted earlier, that, as the *New York Times* report had it, amounted to a targeted "rebuke of China." One remark picked on China for obstructing the freedom of navigation. The other was a straightforward accusation of China's violation of international law in the SCS. So far as we know, however strangely, China did not give any direct feedback, much less a rebuttal, to these serious charges (or similar ones made by other U.S. officials or media gurus), not counting its blanket brush-offs. The self-withdrawal attitude underlining this weird silence is typical of China's usual reaction to international criticisms, even totally unjustified ones. One analyst, Paul Denlinger,

[24] "Vietnam Accuses China in Seas Dispute," *BBC News*, May 30, 2011.

[25] *China Digital Times* (China). http://chinadigitaltimes.net/2011/08/anti-china-protests-continue-in-vietnam-despie-police-opposition/; retrieved November 16, 2011, online.

[26] Tim Taylor, "The Rights Stuff in Oil Islands Row," *The Lawyer*, October 15, 2012.

describes this Chinese practice as a deliberate policy of not responding directly to Western and Western-media criticisms, especially on the SCS question. The reason, he speculates, is that "this policy will expose the Western criticism as ultimately useless, because it does not change the facts on the ground." The Chinese government, he adds, "is aware that some people, and the Western media especially, will criticize it no matter what it does, so why bother with what they say?"[27]

My view on this point, while not in disagreement, is more nuanced, on two counts. At the more intellectual level, I believe in the Enlightenment tradition that truth is to be found through skeptical inquiry and debate, not to be ignored or brushed aside. And, at the more practical level, I think China's silence is in effect self-deluding. The criticisms, no matter how egregious, will not go away simply by ignoring them. The repeated charges of China breaking international law, when repeatedly leveled by foreign governments (the United States and Japan included) — even if prompted more by political motives and formulated more on ideological grounds than true considerations of the merits — may end up shaping the views, nay, poisoning the minds, of even some of our best scholars, the professionals sworn to being guided by reason and faith in the Enlightenment tradition.[28] The resultant nebulous scofflaw stigma hanging over China's head, when repeated so many times and magnified by the Chinese self-deluding oblivion, is bound to destruct China's good name beyond repair. It is something that China can ill afford to live with if it seeks to be recognized, as it earnestly does, as a responsible great nation in its phenomenal second rise.[29]

---

[27] Paul Denlinger, "Will China Do Something to Defend Their Position about the South China Sea?," *Quora*, July 19, 2016, http://www.linkedin/pauldenlinger.

[28] One example is, in an otherwise sensible essay on Trump's approach to China, a respectable Sinologist succumbed to the influence of these repeated questionable charges, when she began by noting: "In recent years, China … *has defied international law* and risked violent clashes in East and South China Seas" (emphasis added). Susan Shirk, "Trump and China," *Foreign Affairs*, vol. 96, no. 2 (March/April 2017): 20.

[29] I have dealt with China's first rise, during 713–1820, when it had the world's largest GDP, based on data meticulously kept by English economic historian Angus Maddison; and its current ascent is its second rise. Hsiung, *China into Its Second Rise* (Singapore: World Scientific, 2012).

Hence, the following discourse, following the Enlightenment spirit, is given in the spirit of searching for true answers through a matter-of-fact inquiry that drills into the two typical charges made by Secretary Clinton above, which are often repeated, almost by rote, by other U.S. (and Japanese) government officials. In doing this, I am guided by one thought: Just visualize an unbending Professor of International Law finding himself in a lecture hall at the legendary Hague Academy of International Law, when he has to respond to questions raised by his lawyer students in the audience. The complex questions put to him might run thusly: Do the facts (and law) known to us warrant (a) the United States' self-assumed right to enforce the freedom of navigation against China in the SCS, and (b) the veracity of the U.S. charge that China is violating international law in its 9-dash-line claim over the SCS waters?

Answer: By examining the evidences, we find that the true picture that can be put together is one which shows that between the United States and China, the ships of one country shadowing those of the other in the SCS is a frequent reciprocal occurrence. And the U.S. side pursues a strategy of armed patrol, despite its questionable legal justification (see below).[30] By comparison, more deadly ships were found on the U.S. side, simply because the U.S. navy is more powerful than the Chinese one. This stark contrast prompted Robert D. Kaplan to conclude that "The U.S. navy presently dominates the South China Sea."[31] Sailing with the 97,000-ton aircraft carrier USS Carl Vinson, out in the SCS on maritime "routine operations," was the guided-missile destroyer USS Wayne E. Meyer, according to a statement issued by the U.S. Navy. The Carl Vinson carried a flight group of more than 60 aircraft, including F/A-18 jet fighters. The operation came amid growing tensions between the United States and China over territory and trade, and, *a fortiori*, as the Trump Administration

[30] Consider: (a) "Chinese Ship Shadows U.S. Carrier," *CNN News*, June 15, 2016 and (b) "U.S. Carrier Starts to Patrol the South China Sea," *CNN News*, February 20, 2017.

[31] Robert D. Kaplan, *Asia's Cauldron: The South China Sea and the End of a Stable Pacific* (New York: Random House, 2015), p. 14.

looked set to take a more confrontational stance toward China than did the previous administrations. During his Senate confirmation hearing, furthermore, new Secretary of State Rex Tillerson blurted out that China should be blocked from accessing the artificial islands it had built, setting the stage for a potential showdown.[32]

Tillerson's statement, wittingly or not, echoed the first of Secretary Hillary Clinton's charges earlier, alleging China's obstruction of the freedom of navigation. The true answer to this allegation, so far as we can see, is twofold. First, there is no hard evidence that China was blocking freedom of navigation in the SCS. The only previous glaring instance that came readily to mind was when two Chinese Air Force jet fighters intercepted a U.S. spy plane (EP-3) on April 1, 2001. But it happened to what even the American side admitted was a plane on an espionage (euphemistically termed "reconnaissance") mission, 70 miles off the coast of China's Hainan Province, or 100 miles from the Chinese military installation in the Paracel Islands in the SCS, when the EP-3 was intercepted.[33] A spy plane on an espionage mission, as such, can hardly claim that its flight qualified as "innocent passage," nor could it claim to be showing "due regard" for the security or sensibility of the coastal State being spied upon, breaching the requirements of the modern law of the sea. Hence, the 2001 incident could not be classified as a case of China's obstruction of the freedom of navigation, including that of air flight, in the SCS.[34] Second, in respect of the new Secretary of State Tillerson's stated policy stance to block China's access to the artificial islands it had constructed, there is nothing in international law (customary law or treaty law) that purports to disallow and ban island building in the high seas by any State. Article 60 (8) of UNCLOS III only states that artificial islands "do not possess the status of islands" and, as such, "they do not have territorial sea of their own." And, a few lines earlier,

---

[32] "U.S. Carrier Starts to Patrol the South China Sea," *CNN News*, February 20, 2017.

[33] See "The Hainan Incident," *Wikipedia*, the free encyclopedia.

[34] A similar case involving the interception of a U.S. spy plane by Chinese jets took place in June 2016, but that was in the East China Sea. *Wall Street Journal*, June 8, 2016.

Art. 60 (6) provides: "All [foreign] ships … shall comply with generally accepted standards regulating navigation in the vicinity of artificial islands …" This clause equally applies to U.S. ships,[35] which are obligated, under Art. 60 (6), to respect Chinese ships' right of access to the China-built artificial islands, notwithstanding Secretary Tillerson's expressed wishes to the contrary.

Critics may fault China for seizing a U.S. underwater drone in December 2016, alleging it was an instance of defiance for the United States' freedom of navigation, although China later returned its capture to the American side. The Pentagon said the underwater vehicle was an unclassified piece of equipment conducting unnamed "routine operations." The official *Renmin ribao* (People's Daily) in Beijing, however, said the drone was "just the tip of the iceberg" in U.S. surveillance on China.[36] If this allegation was true, then the Chinese act of capturing and promptly returning of the drone was probably more an act of showing its displeasure at the U.S. surveillance operation than one calculated to challenge the United States on navigation freedom in the waters of the SCS.

Furthermore, nothing in international law (either customary law, or treaty law) would endow any particular State with the right to play the role of maritime police in the oceans. The United States' self-appointed role in patrolling the SCS and its vocal threat to deny Chinese access to the artificial islands they built remains on shaky legal grounds. Much less can it be justified by alleging a (flimsy) prior Chinese breach of international law as a protective pretext, such as Secretary Hillary Clinton apparently attempted to do. Piracy or seaborne terrorism would be a totally different matter, as a legal ground justifying intervention by the United States, but neither crime can be empirically linked to China.

Here is a good cut-in point to get back to the second charge made by Secretary Hillary Clinton earlier, to the effect that in making its

---

[35] Though it has not ratified the UNCLOS, the United States has declared that it is, nevertheless, committed to observe its provisions.

[36] *CNN News*, December 18, 2016.

9-dash-line claim to the SCS, China is violating international law. The answer is clear but will take a little explanation.

An absolute majority of the arguments against China in the legal debates about the competing SCS claims has been fixated on the islands, but not the waters surrounding them. By contrast, China's claim, if examined from the standpoint of general international law, can be cast in an entirely different mode, that of a historic title over these waters. As we will see in later chapters, China's recorded involvement in the SCS dated as far back as the second century BC, an era before the arrival of the legal concepts later developed in international law, following the Westphalia Conference of 1648, which ushered in the modern system of nation-states. Ancient Chinese annals showed that in the 2nd century BC, envoys dispatched by Emperor Wu of the Han Dynasty (漢武帝) sailed through the confines of the SCS, on their missions to establish contacts with foreign lands on the Sea's periphery and beyond. And, in the year 110 BC, Emperor Wu established two prefectural governments (郡 *jun*) to administer the "vast reaches" (疆域 *jiangyu*) of the SCS.

Similar episodes were recorded in subsequent Chinese annals, including the celebrated seafaring missions headed by (Admiral) Zheng He (or Cheng Ho) during the early 15th century (1405–1433), sailing through the SCS onward to the Indian Ocean, until reaching East Africa after going through Hormuz Strait. Zheng's sizable fleet of 250 mammoth ships and 27,000 men, including professional soldiers (sailors) and medical and other personnel, first passed from Vietnam and other points in Southeast Asia, then proceeded onward to points in South Asia, and so on.[37]

In the *Guangdong tongzhi* (廣東通志 Canton Gazette) published in 1512, it was recorded that the Xisha (now known as Paracels in English) and Nansha (Spratlys) were officially designated as within

[37] I discussed Zheng's seafaring missions in my *China into Its Second Rise,* and see note 29, p. 52. See also Edward Dreyer, *Zheng He: China and the Oceans in the Early Ming Dynasty, 1405–1433* (New York: Pearson/Longman, 2007).

the national defense perimeter of China[38] (more details with documentation in Chapter 2).

In short, one could implore the proverbial Professor at the legendary Hague Academy of International Law, mentioned earlier, to define the status of the SCS in its relations to the Chinese suzerain, using the language of traditional international law. His answer would, invariably, be that the SCS was China's "historic waters" (more on "historic waters" in Chapter 3), although it is one of the things on which the 1982 Law of the Sea Convention (UNCLOS III) is totally silent. But, the preambular part of UNCLOS III proclaims, *inter alia*: "… matters not regulated by this Convention continue to be governed by the rules and principles of <u>general international law</u>" (emphasis added). As will be shown in Chapter 3, "historic waters" is a principle in general international law (as opposed to treaty law), and has been affirmed in judicial cases.

A working hypothesis of this book is that if "historic waters" as the basis of China's claim can stand up to a rigid testing under general international law, then all the on-going disputes posed by its contenders will be elevated to a different plane, casting the competing claims in a different mode that may help in the search for a way out of the dead heat of the prevailing disputes.

The rest of the book, accordingly, will endeavor to ascertain if our stated hypothesis can be verified under general international law. The answer for now is that whether the abovementioned charge against China made by Secretary Hillary Clinton, and similar ones by others, can be sustained will by necessity depend on the ultimate answer whether our stated hypothesis proves verifiable.

---

[38] For parsimony's sake I shall not give more details than this much, so as not to preempt discussions in Chapter 2. Readers who can read Chinese may consult my article "Nanhai zhi zheng: guojifa yu zhongguo ruhe huwei ziji quanyi [The Disputes over the South China Sea: International Law and How China Can Defend Its Own Rights]," *Zhongguo pinglun* (China Review) (Hong Kong), February 2016 issue, pp. 43–45.

Chapter

2

"China's Caribbean": Competing Claims by the Parties — A Comparison in History and Law

The creative idea of likening China's position vis-à-vis the South China Sea (SCS) to America's position vis-à-vis the Caribbean Sea in the 19th and early 20th centuries came originally from Robert D. Kaplan. "It was," he added, "domination of the Greater Caribbean Basin that gave the United States effective control of the Western Hemisphere."[1] I must hasten to add, though, that even until today, the U.S. control of the Caribbean remains unchallenged, unlike China's besieged leadership over the SCS region. The difference, I surmise, is due to the fact that with the sole exception of Cuba, the Caribbean is not populated by states nearly as formidable or assertive as some of the states that loom on the periphery of the SCS. One commonality, admittedly, is that states in both regions, the SCS and

[1] Robert D. Kaplan, *Asia's Cauldron: The South China Sea and the End of a Stable Pacific* (New York, NY: Random House Trade Paperbacks, 2015), p. 13.

the Caribbean, are postcolonial creations. However, in the Caribbean, there are no likes of Vietnam and the Philippines, both of which could count on the support of the U.S. superpower in their disputes with China. The Philippines even has an alliance treaty with the United States, a feature not similarly found among the Caribbean states. None of the latter is allied with a mighty ex-regional patron comparable to the United States.

Another possible reason for the difference, admittedly, is that the United States has not declared sovereignty over the Caribbean Sea; so the 17 nation-states in the area have nothing to rally them together in opposition. Nevertheless, it remains true that a closer look into China's "historic waters" claim over the SCS will discover that the claim is, in the words of one seasoned analyst, "nonexclusive" and "nonexclusionary," as on the matter of the open fishing rights, even oil drilling, in a sea that is only "semienclosed."[2] The vehement reactions to China by Vietnam and the Philippines, among other states, may strike a nonchalant bystander as being out of proportion. In turn, China's "assertive" island building in recent years, in this light, could be viewed as an overreaction to what it had perceived as prior overreactions by these contesting States to China's U-shaped line.

Kaplan's comparison, I might add, serves a heuristic purpose. It reminds us that just like the United States in the Caribbean, China has more stakes in the SCS than does any of its neighbors. It is not hard to imagine that in a discussion of the Caribbean region politics, one is expected to devote more attention to America's stakes and commitments than to the other area states. By the same token, in a discourse on the SCS, it can be argued that China's stakes and claims deserve to be given more space and coverage than the other neighboring states. This is all the more true, considering the challenges to China raised by extraregional powers like the United States, on top of those posed by the indigenous contending parties on the SCS periphery.

---

[2] Sourabh Gupta, "PacNet #88 — Testing China's — and the State Department's — Nine-Dash Line Claims," Center for Strategic and International Studies, December 15, 2014, online.

In this light, we shall begin with China's involvement in the region, delving into a time frame that stretched over two millennium years. We will do so by keeping an eye on reasonable comparisons with the other contending states. To help put things in proper perspective, a brief look at the political geography of the SCS region is in good order.

The SCS: A Political Geography

The SCS is located to the south of China; hence, its name the "South China Sea" by common usage. To the northwest of this body of water are Vietnam and Cambodia, which were under Chinese suzerainty for large parts of history and under French rule from the late 19th century to 1954, under the generic name of (French) Indochina. To the northeast is the Philippines, while the Malay Peninsula and North Borneo — where the tiny sultanate of Brunei finds itself sandwiched in between by two pockets of land that are two component states in the Malaysian federation, known as Sabah and Sarawak — plus the Sumatra Island of Indonesia, are located to the far southern reach of the CSC.

States and territories with borders on the SCS include, following a clockwise direction, the People's Republic of China (PRC) (mainland China), the Republic of China (ROC) (Taiwan), the Philippines, Malaysia, Brunei, Singapore, and Vietnam. Short of this clockwise view, Vietnam is the nearest to China in distance. As many as over 150 islands/islets dot the 1.4 million square miles (3.63 million km) of water that make up the SCS. They are divided by the Chinese government into four island groups for administrative purposes[3]:

1. The Nansha (南沙, Spratly) Archipelago, at 115″ E and 10″ N, is opposite to the Philippines and Borneo

[3] Shao Hsun-cheng, "Chinese Islands in the South China Sea," *People's China* (newspaper), July 1, 1956, pp. 25–27; English translation in Jerome A. Cohen and Hungdah Chiu, eds., *People's China and International Law*, vol. I (Princeton, NJ: Princeton University, 1974), pp. 344–345.

2. The Xisha (西沙, Paracel) Archipelago, at 112″ E, 160″ N, is near China's Hainan Island and Vietnam
3. Zhongsha (中沙, Mcclesfield Bank) Archipelago, at 115″ E and between 15″ and 160″ N, is in the middle, surrounded by the other island groups
4. Dongsha (東沙, Pratas) Archipelago, at 117″ E and 21″ N, is in the north, close to China's Guangdong (Canton) Province

One study shows that, of the many islands claimed by China in the SCS, over forty are actually occupied by foreign countries, with Vietnam taking the largest chunk of 29, followed by the Philippines, 8; and Malaysia, 5.[4]

The ROC (Taiwan), which is in competition with Beijing in claiming the same SCS islands and the adjacent waters, has maintained troops on Itu Abba (太平島), the largest island in the Spratly Island group, since 1956.[5] The PRC (Beijing) has reclaimed more than 3,200 acres (1,295 hectares) of land in the SCS, and built airstrips and equipped its new islands with defensive weaponry, many in the Spratly Island chain.[6]

Other than China (including both the PRC and the ROC), Vietnam probably has a longer history of claim to the SCS than does any of the other neighboring states and territories. Also, it has mounted the fiercest challenge to China in the fight over the Paracel and Spratly Islands in the SCS, as expressed in its May 3, 2011 *note verbale* to the U.N. Secretary General.[7] But it was the Philippines that took the fight to arbitration, in 2014–2016 (discussed in Chapter 4).

---

[4] I am thankful for this information to Dr. Changchuan Wu, of the New York Forum.

[5] *NOWnews* (Taipei), July 7, 2015.

[6] Christopher Bodeen, "Recent Developments Surrounding the SCS," *Associated Press*, March 13, 2011.

[7] Note Verbale No. 77/HC-2011 from the Permanent Mission of the Socialist Republic of Vietnam to the U.N. Secretary General (May 2, 2011), http://www.un.org/Depts/los/clcs_new/submissions_files/vnm37_09/vnm_2011_re_phlchn.pdf.

China's History of Involvement; and Foreign Interferences and Dissent

Now, let us turn to an assessment of the unmatched, super-long history of China's involvement in the SCS, which underscores the historic basis of its claim. As is explained in the previous chapter, our approach will not focus just on the islands, as did most of the extant discussions on the topic. Instead, our concern is with the full maritime reaches, or the whole region covered by water, enclosing the islands, atolls, coral reefs, and other features; and, ultimately, with how China relates itself to the SCS in like fashion.

In terms of recorded history, China's contacts with the SCS can be traced as far back as the Han Dynasty (202 B.C.–220 A.D.), when its ships sailed across the SCS (known in Chinese as Nanhai, 南海, or "South Sea"), using it as a navigational nexus.[8] If we consult Chinese annals, we will find that according to the *Hanshu dilizhi* (汉书地理志), or the Geographical Gazette in the classical History of the Han Dynasty (*Hanshu*) by the famous ancient historian Ban Gu (班固), stories abound that the envoys of Emperor Wu (汉武帝, reign 140–87 BC) sailed through the "South Sea," on their missions to establish contacts with foreign lands on its periphery and beyond. In the year 110 BC, the same Emperor established in the region two prefectures (*jun,* 郡), named Zhuya (珠崖) and Zan'er (儋耳), whose governments were mandated to administer and watch over the "vast reaches" (*jiangyu*, 疆域) of the SCS.[9] The government seat of the Zhuya

---

[8] As discussed in a number of papers presented at the South China Sea Conference, sponsored by the American Enterprise Institute, September 7–9, 1994, incl. R. Haller-Trost, "International Law and the Claims to the Spratly Islands." Also, Chi-kin Lo, *China's Policy towards Territorial Disputes: The Case of the South China Sea Islands* (London and New York: Routledge, 1989), p. 15. Both were cited in Mark Valencia *et al.*, *Sharing the Resources of the South China Sea* (Honolulu, HI: University of Hawaii, 1997), p. 20, text at reference for note 28.

[9] Cited in my "Nanhai zhi zheng: guojifa yu zhongguo ruhe huwei ziji quanyi [The Disputes over the South China Sea: International Law and How China Can Defend Its Own Rights]," *Zhongguo pinglun* [China Review] (Hong Kong, February 2016), pp. 43–45.

prefecture has come down to become the city of Haikou, the capital of today's Province of Hainan Island, in the Qiongzhou Gulf,[10] at the northern tip of the SCS. (To bring things up to date, in 2010, China named the Sansha City on Hainan Island as the administrative center for the SCS.)

As from 111 BC, China began to dispatch naval patrol ships to the SCS, commanded by Admiral Yang Pu, with 100,000 sailors under him, on patrol missions.[11]

History annals for later periods show that Chinese voyages to the region increased in frequency during the powerful Tang Dynasty (618–906 AD).[12] During the North Song (Sung) Dynasty (960–1127 AD), Chinese naval patrols reached the Xisha (Paracel) Islands. The *Wu Jing Jong Yao* (Outline of Military Affairs) recorded that the Court "ordered patrols by imperial forces and the building of barracks for the naval patrols" in Guangnan (now Guangdong), "commissioning the building of keeled sea-faring warships" which could reach Jiuruluozhou in seven days, sailing in a southwestern direction from Tunmenshan with a fair east wind. Jiuruluozhou was the ancient name for today's Xisha (Paracel) Islands. The dispatch of naval warships to patrol its territories illustrated that the North Song (Sung) Court already had Xisha Islands under its jurisdiction.[13] Similar activities were recorded for the Southern Song (Sung) Dynasty (1127–1279).[14]

---

[10] According to information available at www.hq.xinhuanet.com/x, and en.wiktionary.org/wiki/珠崖.

[11] S. Yeh, "Nansha fengyun he guoji gongfa [Nansha Imbroglio and International Law]," 19 *EcOn & L* 27 (1988), cited in Te-Kuang Chang, "China's Claim of Sovereignty over Spratly and Paracel Islands: A Historical and Legal Perspective," *Case Western Reserve Journal of International Law*, vol. 23, no. 3 (1991): 5.

[12] Ning Lu, *The Spratly Archipelago: The Origins of the Claims and Possible Solutions* (Washington, DC: International Center, 1993), 27f; cited in Valencia, see note 8, p. 61 and note 27.

[13] "China's Indisputable Sovereignty over the Xisha and Nansha Islnds," Document of the PRC Foreign Ministry (1980).

[14] As seen in Zhou Qufei, *Lingnan duida* [Colloquey from the Lingnan Studio] (published in 1178).

In Chapter 1, we made references to (Admiral) Zheng He's (Cheng Ho, 郑和) seafaring missions (1405–1433) during the Ming Dynasty that sailed through the SCS, on their journey to the Indian Ocean and beyond, taking them to 30 countries. In every journey, the escorting Chinese navy passed through the Nansha (Spratly) Islands. His three interpreters each wrote a book about the Nansha Islands. Thus, some of the islands in the group were named in memory from these exploratory missions, such as Tizard Bank and Reefs, Flat Island, Nansha Island, Loaita Bank and Reefs, Lankiam Cay, and Sin Cowo Island.[15] The maps drawn from these missions, known as Zheng He Hanghai Tu (郑和航海图, Maps from Zheng He's Seafaring Missions), identified the various SCS islands by name and by their specific locations and features.[16] The Guangdong Tongzhi (广东通志, Canton Gazette) published in 1512, listed the Xisha (Paracel) and Nansha (Spratly) Islands as within China's national-defense perimeters. In the same vein, the Haifang Jiyao (海防辑要, Maritime Defense Digest), published in 1830, identified these same islands as the "vital strategic points" in China's frontier security.[17]

As Western legal concepts like "sovereignty" were unknown to the Chinese until more modern times, we cannot apply the word "sovereignty" to China's claim to the SCS in its long history of involvement, which included its experiences of administering the SCS region through the prefectures of Zhu Yai (珠崖), Zhan Er (儋耳), and Qiongzhou (琼州), mentioned earlier. A more adequate way of describing this Chinese involvement may be to call it the exercise of Chinese "influence" or, using a typically Chinese concept, "authority" over the SCS region. To use a more culturally neutral term, we may call it Chinese "presence." In fact, Chinese presence in the Spratlys is more consistently documented from the 19th century

[15] Jon M. Van Dyke and Dale L. Bennett, "Islands and the Delimitation of Ocean Space in the South China Sea," *Ocean Yearbook*, vol. 10, (1993): 62, cited in Valencia *et al.*, *Sharing the Resources*, p. 21.

[16] Ibid., p. 63.

[17] Also cited in Hsiung, see note 9, p. 44.

onward. Tomb stones and household utensils from Emperor Tongzhi's reign (同治, 1862–1875) of the Qing Dynasty have been found on the island.[18]

During the Ming and Qing (1644–1911) dynasties, the Xisha and Nansha Islands were under the administration of Wanzhou, in Qiongzhou Prefecture (琼州) (now Wanning and Lingshu counties of the Hainan Province).[19]

The first ever act of making a sovereign claim by the Chinese happened in 1876, when China's Ambassador to England claimed the Paracels as Chinese territory. And, in the same year, a German survey team on the Spratly Islands was expelled by the Chinese for intrusion into China's territory.[20]

Although in traditional times China never used the term "sovereignty," its exercise of authority in the region was never seriously challenged until after the Sino-French war of 1884. Following the Tientsin (Tianjin) Treaty of 1885, which legally ended the war and formalized China's loss of Annam (today's Vietnam), France and China concluded in 1887, a Convention Concerning the Delimitation of the Border Between China and Tonkin. If the later independent Vietnam after shaking off French colonial rule should try to lay claims to islands in SCS by invoking this Treaty, it would find itself confronting a stupendous problem, because both the French and the Chinese sides later disagreed on what exactly were agreed upon, even on the question whether the treaty delimited any parts of the SCS itself. I know the existence of an old Chinese document that contained the Qing Empire's position which amounted to a concrete evidence of what may be a most revealing part in the "legislative history" of the 1887 Convention. The key statement in the document was that the Chinese side would agree only to the delimitation of the land (the border between China and Tonkin), but not the delimitation of

[18] Van Dyke and Bennet, see note 15.

[19] Document of PRC Foreign Ministry, see note 12.

[20] Van Dyke and Bennett, Ocean Yearbook, p. 63.

the SCS itself.[21] This may be the reason why no names of any islands were mentioned in the convention. Thus, the convention should not be cited as a vitiation of the Chinese claims with respect to the SCS, as one analyst tried to do.

Nevertheless, France in the 1930s made a formal claim to seven of the larger Spratly features, and to some extent exercised actual physical control of the Spratly Islands.[22] The episode took place at a time when China (still under Chiang Kai-shek's government) was fully engrossed with fighting the Japanese invasion that began with the occupation of Shenyang (Mukden) by the Japanese Kwantung Army in 1931, leading to the eight-year War of Resistance (1937–1945); hence it would not be able to direct its attention to the French encroachments in the SCS.

By the late 1930s, Japan's Imperial Army had established a strong presence in the SCS. Its interest in the region had begun since 1917, when a Japanese company started exploiting some of the guano deposits on the Spratly islets. The Japanese used Itu Aba (太平島), the largest in the Spratly Island group, as a submarine basing area to intercept shipping through the region.[23] The Japanese occupation lasted until 1945, at the end of World War II, when the Japanese exited the region.

Cynical critics of China often seized upon these temporal breaks in its hold on the SCS islands as a pretext for "weakening," if not nullifying, the Chinese claim based on its long history of control. But, these critics are obviously only partially informed on the international law of territorial acquisition and maintenance. In the classic *Island of Palmas* case (1928), decided by a PCA tribunal, it was

---

[21] See LI Jinming, "zhongfa kanjie douzheng yu beibuwan haiyu huajie [The Sino-French Border Demarcation Dispute and the Question on the Delimitation of the Northern Part of the Sea]," Studies of South Sea Issues, no. 2 (2000).

[22] R. Haller-Trost, "International Law and the Claims to the Spratly Islands" (paper given at the South China Sea Conference, Washington, DC: American Enterprise Institute, 1994), p. 13; cited in Valencia *et al.*, *Sharing the Resources of the South China Sea*, p. 21.

[23] Haller-Trost, International Law and the Claims to the Spratly Islands, 15, 28.

shown that (a) effective control must follow discovery to establish territorial sovereignty, hence the Dutch claim was superior to that of the Spaniards, whose discovery not followed by effective control could establish only an "inchoate title"; and (b) once established, sovereignty need not be adversely affected even by "considerable gaps" in the "evidence of continuous display of sovereign control." After noting that between 1666 and 1906 no state contested Dutch sovereignty, the arbitral award, rendered by Max Huber, the arbitrator, concluded that "the Netherlands title of sovereignty, acquired by continuous and peaceful display of State authority during a long period of time going probably back beyond the year 1700, therefore, holds good," despite the considerable breaks in the Netherlands hold on the island.[24]

Hence, criticisms that the above "breaks" in the 1930s, caused by the French and the Japanese intrusions, contributed to the "weakening" of China's claim to the SCS is unconvincing and implausible, in light of the law as clarified in the classical *Island of Palmas* case.

Cynics were also fond of making a mount out of an anthill with Article 2 of the San Francisco Peace Treaty (SFPT) signed in 1951, by which Japan only renounced all "right, title, and claim to . . . the Spratly Islands and Paracel Islands," among other territories, without explicitly assigning them to any recipient country.[25] Hence, these cynics concluded that China's position alleging that this Art. 2 of the SFPT proved the legitimacy of its historical title to the Spratly and Paracel Islands was, in their opinion, not credible. The best refutation of this cynical view, however, came from Sourahb Gupta, an Indian analyst at the Institute for China-America Studies (ICAS), a think tank in Washington, DC.[26]

---

[24] Island of Palmas Case (U.S. v. The Netherlands), PCA, 1928, in 2 *U.N. Reports on Arbitral Awards*, 829ff.

[25] San Francisco Treaty of Peace, September 8, 1951; 136 UNTS 1832.

[26] Sourabh Gupta, "Alternative Facts and the Threat in the South China Sea," *East Asia Forum*, February, 14, 2017.

After acknowledging that the Unites States, for decades, had not taken any position on the sovereign issue in the SCS, Gupta noted that "on the only occasion that it did throw its diplomatic weight behind a claimant, the [U.S.] State Department and its advisor, John Foster Dulles, came down on the side of the Chinese." In a separate treaty with the ROC (unofficially known as the "Taipei Treaty"), signed at the United States' behest on the day the SFPT came into force, April 1, 1952, Japan was made to renounce its holdings on, among other territories, the Spratly and Paracel Islands (Art. 2), he pointed out.[27] This separate treaty was necessary since the State of China was not invited by the United States to the San Francisco conference, for a practical reason. The United States, at the time continued to recognize the ROC after its retreat to Taiwan in 1949 after losing the civil war, but did not recognize the PRC, despite the latter's effective control of the entire China mainland. Washington was understandably undecided as to which of the two regimes should be invited to represent the whole of China.

Unlike the multilateral SFPT, the "Taipei Treaty" was a bilateral instrument. Hence, as one party (Japan) renounced the named islands, then the same islands *ipso facto* reverted to the treaty's other party (ROC/Taiwan). The only uncertainty, from the standpoint of legal precision, is whether the Chinese government seated in Beijing can make its claim to the islands on the strength of this 1952 ROC–Japan treaty. That should be a matter to be ironed out between the two Chinese regimes. Nevertheless, I would add that the ROC (Taipei), at the time of 1952, was recognized as representing the State of China by all countries that recognized it, including the United States and Japan. Despite its nickname ("Taipei Treaty"), the instrument should be considered, from the standpoint of both diplomatic practice and international law, as a treaty between the State of China and Japan. In addition, I would further note that under Art. 5 of the bilateral treaty, Japan renounced "all special rights and interests in China," which would include the rights and

[27] ROC–Japan Peace Treaty of 1952, 138 UNTS 38.

interests associated with Japan's occupation of the SCS islands from the 1930s up to 1945. Hence, these islands reverted back to China, the other signatory of the bilateral treaty, beyond the shadow of a doubt.

Putting aside the 1952 ROC–Japan treaty, as Gupta noted, the PRC could trace its claim, for the recovery of the said SCS islands, to the wartime Cairo and Potsdam Declarations, as was confirmed in Art. 3 of the PRC's 1972 normalization agreement (ersatz peace treaty) with Japan. The legal significance of Gupta's point is attested to by the fact that "no other regional claimant can produce a [similar] Spratly and Paracel renunciation or reversion clause in its own post-war normalization agreement with Tokyo."[28]

Interestingly enough, in 2016, both Beijing and Taipei separately celebrated the 70th anniversary of the return of the SCS islands as from 1946, following the end of World War II. Taiwan held an "Exhibition Commemorating the 70th Anniversary of the Recovery of the South China Sea Islands," at Academia Historica, which co-organized the event with the ROC Ministry of Internal Affairs (MOI).[29] In mainland China, a grand exhibition was staged in the Provincial Museum on Hainan Island, under the joint auspices of four organizations, including the Chinese Oceanic Council. And, on that occasion, Beijing reiterated that the islands were recovered to China under the aegis of the Cairo and Potsdam Declarations,[30] which Japan accepted in the Instrument of Surrender it signed on September 2, 1945 on the U.S.S. Missouri.

There was no dearth of disputation by the other contending claimants to China's claim over the SCS islands, for example, by the Republic of Vietnam (ROV) (before 1975),[31] the Socialist Republic

---

[28] Gupta, see note 25.

[29] "South China Sea: Taiwan to Uphold Sovereignty in South China Sea," *Taipei Times*, December 10, 2016.

[30] *HINEWS*, March 8, 2016.

[31] South Vietnam became the Republic of Vietnam in 1954, when it separated from French colonial rule, until its collapse after U.S. withdrawal in 1975.

of Vietnam (SRV) (after 1975),[32] the Philippines and Malaysia. From 1973 to 1988, armed conflicts erupted between Vietnam (as invader) and China (the PRC, as defender). Both Chinese regimes (PRC and ROC) maintained claims that the four major groups of islands in the SCS are solely Chinese territory. As the PRC was commemorating the 70th anniversary of the recovery of the SCS islands, in 2016, as noted earlier, the Vietnamese spared no time in raising a protest. A spokesman of the Vietnamese Foreign Ministry stated that nothing will change Vietnam's "indisputable rights to these islands." Vietnam, he said, protested the Chinese commemoration, because it "could only jeopardize the relations between the two countries."[33]

China's U-Shaped 9-Dash Line: Origins and Legal Significance

As broached in Chapter 1, there are two ways by which to dissect, and tackle, the multiple disputes surrounding the SCS. One, as most studies do, is to focus on who owns what islands. But, thus far, no analyst in this camp has come up with a readily workable legal solution that will settle the disputes bedeviling the competing claimant countries. The other approach, which is our preference, is to broaden our perspective to take into view the whole SCS as a maritime region covered by the reaches of its waters that encompass the islands and all other features within it. This approach invariably leads us to the question, and significance, of "historic waters" in international law. As we suggested in Chapter 1, our hypothesis is that if China's claim based on the postulation that what the 9-dash line encloses in the SCS is its historic waters — mind-boggling as it may sound at first blush — can stand up to a test by the relevant general international law, then

---

[32] After the unification of South Vietnam and North Vietnam in 1975, the country became known as the Socialist Republic of Vietnam.

[33] "Vietnam's Strange Protest to China's Commemoration of the 70th Anniversary of the Recovery of the Paracel and Spratly Islands," Observer.net, December 14, 2016.

everything in the harrying disputes will have a glimmer of hope for a reasonable solution, as we will endeavor to ascertain and explicate in the rest of the book.

Following the French assertion of claims to the Paracels in 1931 and Spratlys in 1933, China decided to respond in defense of its sovereignty in the SCS.[34] A Review Committee for Sea and Land Map was established in June 1933, as a result. After a year-long review by the Committee, the government published the *Zhongguo Nanhai Ge Daoyu Tu* (The Map of China's South China Sea Islands), in April 1935.[35]

During 1946–1947, the ROC MOI conducted a further study of the situation in the SCS and, based on additional information collected by the Chinese navy, published a "Cross Reference Table of the New and Old Terminology [Names] of the South China Sea Islands" in December 1947. The document listed 159 islands/islets in a newly drawn map. Later, the MOI formally issued the 1947 map, known as "The Map of Locations of South China Sea Islands," on which a U-shaped 11-dash line was drawn, encircling the four larger groups of SCS islands, as well as their surrounding waters.[36] Since then, the U-shaped line has been used in all Chinese maps for the purpose of showing the boundary limits of China's maritime areas and its claim to the SCS islands. (See a reproduction of this map, with the U-shaped line, in Chapter 1.) It merits repeating that after 1949, the PRC government eliminated the two dashes closest to the Gulf of Tonkin, as a gesture of friendship for Ho Chi Minh's Vietnam, thus it became a 9-dash line.

[34] Cf. Coon-ho Park, "The South China Sea Disputes: Who Owns the Islands and the Natural Resources," *Ocean Development and International Law Journal*, vol. 5, no. 1 (1978): 33ff.

[35] HAN Jen-hua, ed., *A Compilation of Historic Documents and Materials Relating to the South China Sea Islands* (Beijing: Dongfang Publishers, 1985), pp. 172–179.

[36] Cf. Yann-huei Song and Peter Kien-hong Yu, "China's 'Historic Waters' in the South China Sea: An Analysis from Taiwan, R.O.C.," *American Asian Review* (New York), vol. 12, no. 4 (1994): pp. 83–101.

A sharp eye will notice that the U-shaped line was apparently not drawn with any precision in mind, as it did not give the geographic coordinates. But, it is also true that the line does not purport to claim the entire SCS, as is often alleged by critics with an ax to grind. The apparently sufficient space left in between the U-shaped broken line and the putative coastlines of the surrounding entities on the map, Vietnam, Malaysia, Brunei, and the Philippines, can only imply an allowance for the territorial sea that they each may opt to claim (after they later emerged as independent States from colonial rule).

In the rest of the book, we will have plenty of opportunity to return to the question of the legality of China's claim on the basis of historic waters, and to that of the concept of "historic waters" itself, in the context of general international law. Here, I wish to register two points for their importance in helping tease out the legal issues for our discussions.

1. First, as the 1947 Chinese U-shaped line was announced to the world, it received no immediate protest or complaint from any neighboring state, or Western country with colonies in the region — such as France (in Indochina, incl. Vietnam), Britain (Malaya–Singapore, and Brunei), and the United States (the Philippines). By deduction, it can be said that the Chinese U-shaped line received the acquiescence of the international community. Under a separate heading below, we will briefly review the discernible attitudes of foreign (incl. the colonial) powers on China's claim to the SCS islands and their adjacent waters. This will be followed by a section on the competing claims of the other contesting parties.
2. Second, my other point is really a counter to skeptics who may harbor doubts about whether "historic waters" as a concept in international law has been rendered obsolete under the 1982 U.N. Convention on the Law of the Sea (UNCLOS). These skeptics, indeed, may have found occasion to cheer, when the PCA Arbitral Tribunal issued its 2016 award in the Philippines v.

China case. The award said that the Arbitral Tribunal could find no legal basis (in UNCLOS) for the Chinese claim based on historic waters. Chapter 4 dwells on the legal issues and implications associated with that arbitration case. But, I do not want to leave dangling, for too long, the skeptics' doubt about the legality of the Chinese U-shaped line, when viewed against UNCLOS provisions. The answer is that, while the 1982 Convention does not mention "historic waters" by name, the same idea is nevertheless provided in Article 47 (1):

> An archipelagic State may draw straight archipelagic base-lines joining the outermost points of the outermost islands and drying reefs of the archipelago provided that within such base-lines are included in the main islands and an area in which the ratio of the area of the water to the land, including atolls, is between 1 to 1 and 9 to 1.

While China itself is not an archipelagic state per se, the total area occupied by the various islands in the SCS claimed by China on historic grounds, as demonstrated in the preceding review of a history over two millennia, may arguably constitute a rare archipelagic extension of China. As such, the U-shaped line can thus be considered as resulting from the joining of the "outermost points of the outermost islands and drying reefs," as Art. 47 (1) provides. Likewise, the space left between the broken U line itself and the putative coastlines of the other countries surrounding the line seems to conform to the same Article 47 (1) in allowing the interface of an area in which a certain ratio of the area of the water to the land, including atolls, is kept at reasonable proportions.

The U-shaped line was drawn 35 years before the 1982 Convention. Unless we believe that the map drawer was truly prophetic, the reason why the U line (drawn in 1947) demonstrates so close a conformity with the provision in Art. 47 (1) (of the 1982 Convention) is probably that the architects for both probably followed a common human sense of logic that transcends time and cultures.

To this, I have to hasten to add that notwithstanding the above-mentioned conformity, the U-shaped line does enclose parts of the 200-mile exclusive economic zone (EEZ) that each of the corresponding coastal States is permitted under UNCLOS to claim. Hence, there is a conflict-laden overlapping problem (see map below).

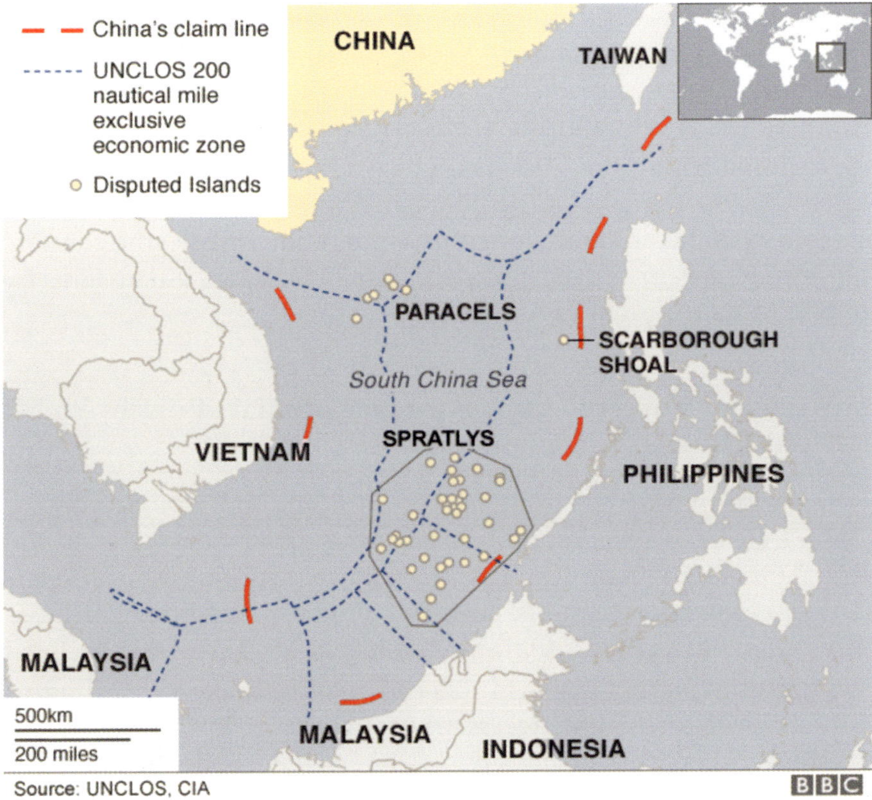

Of course, the EEZ is a new concept unknown in 1947. As will be noted in Chapter 4, following the doctrine of intertemporal law, the legality of the Chinese U-shaped line, formulated in 1947, should be adjudged by the contemporaneous international law of 1947, not the later changed law 35 years hence.

If, however, China's claim of historic waters is sustainable after being tested against general international law (we will find out later), then all features within the U-shaped 9-dash line will be within the Chinese "historic waters." It is not exactly certain whether under international law the legal status of historic waters is analogous to internal waters or territorial waters. A jurist in ROC/Taiwan has argued against imputing an internal-waters characteristic to historic waters.[37] Nor has the PRC made such a claim. But, in a desperate dispute, when push comes to shove, it cannot be ruled out that Beijing might be tempted to make such a claim, making every thing, including the islands and the EEZs claimed by the other States that are enclosed within the U-shaped line, to be within China's internal waters. So, for the sake of the glimmer of a hope in the quest for an amiable workable solution, it might be politically wise for the contesting parties not to let the protest to the U-shaped 9-dash line be pushed to such a point of no return.

Attitudes of Foreign (Incl. Former Colonial) Powers Toward China's SCS Claims

In a study of the reactions of the international community to China's claim of sovereignty over the four groups of islands in the SCS, Te-kuang Chang was able to map the attitudes of a number of major powers, including former colonial powers in Southeast Asia. These attitudes varied quite widely; and can be divided into two groups, roughly between: (a) those states that were willing to show respect for, if not necessarily to accept, China's claim; and (b) those others that professed a preference to challenge China by disputing its claim, or by taking action, even occupying the islands.[38]

[37] Kuen-Chen Fu, *Nan (zhongguo) hai falv diwei zhi yanjiu* (Legal Status of the South (China) Sea) (Taipei, 1995), p. 33.
[38] Te-kuang Chang, *Case Western Reserve Journal of International Law*, 399ff.

Britain

As a whole, Britain showed a rather positive attitude toward China's claims. A senior British diplomat on January 21, 1974 recalled that in 1957, London sent a note to the PRC in which Britain impliedly recognized Chinese sovereignty over the Pratas (Dongsha) and Paracels (Xisha) islands. Later, in the British Parliament's 1985 Sub-Committee report, Sir Peter Blachen, Chairman of the Committee on Hong Kong Affairs, mentioned that China included SCS islands as Chinese territory; and no foreign country raised any objection. But, it added, since research showed evidence of plenty of petroleum and mineral potentials in the SCS, the neighboring states began to become involved.[39]

Germany

In 1883, as noted before, a German team surveyed the Nansha (Spratly) islands; but it abandoned the survey after the Chinese Government protested. In so doing, Germany showed what in international law is known as implied recognition of, or acquiescence to, China's sovereignty.[40]

The United States

The U.S. government, as already noted in Chapter 1, has staked out an official position of noninvolvement as to claims of sovereignty in the SCS. In Art. 3 of the U.S.–Spain Peace Treaty, the Philippine Islands ceded by Spain did not include the Spratlys. The *World Geographical Names Encyclopedia*, published in New York jointly by the Columbia University Press and the American National Geographical

[39] AP News, London, January 21, 1974; Hong Kong Dongfang Daily News, September 23, 1985. The Nansha islands are known in English as the Spratly islands, because they are named after the British captain Spratly who mapped them in the 1880s.

[40] Yeh, see note 10, 28.

Society, listed the Paracel and Spratly Islands as Chinese territories, with the following statement: "Paracel Islands and Spratly Islands of China belong to the part of the Guangdong Province. Prior to World War II, they were controlled by the French. From 1939 to 1945, they were under Japanese occupation. After World War II, they were returned to China."[41]

The Soviet Union

Moscow always recognized Chinese sovereignty over the Paracel and Spratly Islands. The 1967 *Soviet World Map*, put out by the Council of Ministers' Publication, and the 1973 *Soviet Encyclopedia*, plus the *Ocean Map* published by the Ministry of National Defense, all indicated that the Nansha and Xisha Islands were Chinese territories.[42]

The Soviet Union, at the 1951 San Francisco conference on the Japanese Peace Treaty, objected to the Saigon regime's attempt to claim the Nansha and Xisha Islands, and argued instead that these islands belonged to China, which was absent at the conference.[43]

France

As also noted before, France occupied the Nansha (Spratly) Islands in 1933, when China was preoccupied with its struggle against Japanese aggression which began two years before. The Chinese Government lodged a strong protest to France and cited the 1887 Sino-French Convention on the boundary line between China and the French-ruled Vietnam. The convention indicated that the Paracel and Spratly Islands were outside the boundary line of Vietnam. The Chinese Government also pointed to a French Government Bulletin issued on July 25, 1933, which stated that only Chinese lived on these islands, contrary to the French verbal claim that there were no Chinese on the islands; and that the Bulletin indicated that the Nansha Islands

---

[41] Ibid.

[42] *People's Daily* (Beijing), January 22, 1974.

[43] Yeh, see note 10, 28.

belonged to China. The French were unable to present any reasonable counterargument, and after World War II, never again contested the matter.[44]

Competing Claims by the Other Contestants

Competing claims have come mainly from Vietnam, the Philippines, Malaysia, and even Brunei, if we leave out the ROC (Taiwan) whose claim is peculiar by dint of the simultaneous existence of two Chinese regimes. Hence, their claims duplicate (and in some ways reinforce) each other, which in a quiet way also demonstrates that the idea of One China is a reality, not so "preposterous" a "fudge" as *The Economist* (3/11/21017, p. 13) made it out to be.

The Vietnamese Position

We should keep in mind that 1975 marks a line of division. Before that year, the country was divided into North and South Vietnam. The South, known as the ROV, lasted from 1954 to 1975. North Vietnam descended from the part of colonial Vietnam that shook off colonial rule early to become an independent state in 1945 under Ho Chi Minh; and was known as the Democratic Republic of Vietnam (DRVN), with its capital in Hanoi. After the North unified the South militarily in 1975, the unified country assumed the name of SRV. The attitudes of Vietnam, before and after 1975, were very different and have to be discussed separately.

The ROV's attitude

The ROV (South Vietnam) started with a legal argument, and followed with military action, in its challenge to China's claim of sovereignty over the SCS. It landed troops on some of the islands in the Paracel and Spratly groups. For instance, South Vietnam took possession of the Crescent Islands in 1955, and occupied it until the Battle

[44] Ibid.

of the Paracel Islands with China in January 1974, when its troops were driven out by the Chinese, who then took them back.

A document issued by the ROV on July 30, 1971, known as the "Declaration on the Sovereignty of the Republic of Vietnam over the Archipelagos of Paracels and Spratlys," listed five points in support of its sovereignty claim, as follows:

1. In 1802, Emperor Gia Long created a "Dio Hoang Sa" (Company of the Paracels) to supervise the exploitation of these islands.
2. In 1830, under Emperor Minh Mang, the "Truong Sa" (Spratly) Islands were included as part of Vietnamese territory on the first maps published by the kingdom.
3. In 1930 and 1933, acting on behalf of the Vietnamese empire, the French government officially took possession of the Spratly Islands and notified foreign powers of its possession by a letter dated September 29, 1933.
4. During the 1951 San Francisco Peace Conference, Japan had to renounce all of the territories it had taken by force during the Second World War, including the Spratly and Paracel Islands. The Vietnamese delegate to the conference made a public statement of Vietnamese sovereignty over the Paracels and Spratly Islands. The statement aroused no objections from any of the 51 powers represented at the peace conference.
5. On October 22, 1956, the president of the ROV placed the Spratly Islands under the administration of the Province of Ba Ria.[45]

The Declaration concluded: "The Republic of Vietnam remains the only power to possess the most legitimate rights of sovereignty over the Archipelagos of Spratly and Paracel because it has fulfilled the

[45] ROV Document "Sovereignty of the Republic of Vietnam over the Spratly and Paracel Islands," February 5, 1974.

conditions required by the convention of 1885 concerning the establishment of territorial competency."[46]

The socialist republic of Vietnam

The position of the SRV is inconsistent. Prior to the unification of North and South Vietnam in 1975, the DRVN (North Vietnam) recognized Chinese sovereignty over Xisha (Paracel) and Nansha (Spratly) Islands, without dispute. On June 15, 1956, Vice Foreign Minister Un Van Khiem of DRVN, told the Chinese *charge d'affairs ad interim*, Li Zhimin, that "according to Vietnamese data, the Xisha and Nansha islands are historically part of Chinese territory." Le Loc, Acting Director of the Asian Department in the Vietnamese Foreign Ministry, was present at the meeting and, citing specific Vietnamese data, confirmed that "judging from history, these islands were already part of China at the time of the Song dynasty [960–1279]."[47]

In a declaration issued on September 4, 1958, the PRC government announced that the breath of China's territorial sea extended 12 nautical miles from its coastlines, and that this rule applied to all Chinese territories, including Nansha (Spratlys), Xisha (Paracels), Dongsha (Pratas), and Zhongsha (Mcclesfield Bank) Islands in the SCS. Two days later, on September 6, Nhan Dan, the official organ of the Vietnamese Workers (Communist) Party prominently featured on its front page details of the Chinese government declaration.

In a note dated September 14, DRVN Prime Minister Pham Van Dong reassured his Chinese counterpart, Premier Zhou Enlai that "the government of the Democratic Republic of Vietnam recognizes and supports the declaration of the government of the People's Republic of China on China's territorial sea made on September 4, 1958."[48] In view of the specific part of the Chinese declaration that stated that the Chinese territories to be effected by the 12-mile

---

[46] Ibid.

[47] H. Chen, "Anchao xiongyong di nansha xingshi [The Gathering Storm over the Nansha Situation]," *Central Daily News* (Taipei), November 16, 1988, 1.

[48] The original letter of Premier Pham Van Dong is reprinted in Chapter 1.

territorial sea rule included the four named SCS archipelagos, the official DRVN's expressed acceptance and support clearly signified a recognition that these named island groups in the SCS were Chinese territories.

However, after the unification of Vietnam, in 1975, the SRV, which is actually the successor to the DRVN (North Vietnam) before, reverted to an earlier Vietnamese position claiming Hoang Sa (Vietnamese for Paracels) and Truang Sa (Spratlys) Islands to be Vietnamese territories.[49]

Before we get to the other countries' competing claims, I should pause to offer my brief evaluation of the validity and truthfulness of the Vietnamese claims as given by both ROV and SRV governments.

First, the position of ROV (South Vietnam). In one of the five points it listed, the ROV document mentioned earlier, the Declaration of July 30, 1971, recalled what transpired at the San Francisco Conference of 1951. It said that when the Vietnamese delegate to the conference made a public statement on Vietnamese sovereignty over the Paracels and Spratly Islands, it "aroused no objections from any of the 51 powers represented at the peace conference." Without checking any further, we have seen earlier that this Vietnamese claim was at once contradicted by the Soviet delegate on the spot, to the effect that these islands belonged to China.[50]

Furthermore, another point made in the ROV's declaration traced to 1802 as the earliest time when Vietnamese King Gia Long created a company to supervise the exploitation of the resources of the Hoang Sa (Paracel) Islands. In 1803, it added, under Emperor Minh Mang, the Throng Sa (Spratly) Islands were "included as part of the

---

[49] See Te-kuang Chang, see note 37, 419. Moreover, In Chapter 1, we noted that when in 2014 the Chinese placed an oil rig in the territorial waters of Xisha (Paracel) island, which Premier Pham Van Dong's letter would have recognized as within Chinese territory, the SRV government protested vehemently to China, and Vietnamese mobs even staged violent rioting, ransacking, and torching of Chinese factors and companies, and so on.

[50] See the text above at reference for note 39; also as noted in Yeh, see note 11, p. 28.

Vietnamese territory on the first maps published by the kingdom." Considering the fact that for several periods in history, lasting for 600 years at the longest and 20 years at the shortest, Annam (today's Vietnam) was within the bailiwick of the Chinese empire, before it came under French colonial rule in 1887,[51] the year 1802 may indeed be very early for a free and independent Vietnamese kingdom in history. But, when compared with the recorded historical roots, noted earlier, of Chinese involvement with the SCS, going back to the Han Dynasty (206–220 BC), followed by the establishment of two Chinese prefectures to administer the SCS region in 110 BC, and the Chinese troops patrolling of the region beginning in 111 BC, and so on., the Vietnamese claim tracing a beginning back to 1802 at the earliest, cannot but pale by the side of what China can claim on the ground of historicity. I shall not belabor the obvious point, except to note that the so-called "first maps published by the [Vietnamese] kingdom" in 1830 likewise lose their thunder when compared with the Chinese Zhenghe Seafaring Maps published in the 15th century, also noted before.

In another one of the five points made in the above ROV Declaration, the French occupation of the Spratlys in 1933 was mentioned as an episode in support of Vietnam's claim. What it did not mention was that in China's protest on the occasion, the Chinese, to reiterate, pointed to a French Government Bulletin, issued on July 25, 1933, which stated that only Chinese lived on these islands, admitting that they were Chinese territories; and the French could not find any counterargument in reply.

Second, the changed position in post-1975 SRV. The SRV did not offer any substantive reason why it abandoned its position and reverted to an earlier one that had claimed the Paracel and Spratly Islands to be Vietnamese territory. The only clue was that the year 1958 fell in a time frame when DRVN had to depend on China's support for its war against the United States.[52] To translate it into legal

---

[51] For this part of the history, see "Annam," Wikipedia, the free encyclopedia.

[52] Henry J. Kenny, *Shadow of the Dragon: Vietnam's Continuing Struggle with China and the Implications for U.S. Foreign Policy* (Washington, DC: Potomac Books, 2002), pp. 61–64.

language, it means that SRV was pleading "changed circumstances," or *rebus sic stantibus*, as a pretext under international law. If so, SRV would have to answer to the provisions of the Law of Treaties Convention (1969), on whether a change of circumstance can be used to back out from an agreement defining a boundary.[53] Art. 62 (2) of the convention specifically stipulates: "A change of circumstance may not be invoked as a ground for terminating or withdrawing from a treaty: (a) if the treaty establishes a boundary. . . ." (emphasis added). What constitutes a "treaty"? you may ask. According to Art. 1 (a) of the convention, "Treaty means an international agreement concluded between States in written form and governed by international law, whether embodied in a single instrument [including an official letter], or in two or more related instruments and whatever its peculiar designation" (emphasis and bracketed words added). Prime Minister Pham Van Dong's letter (a written single instrument) established Vietnam's acceptance of a boundary between China and his own country, and officially declared Vietnamese acceptance of Chinese sovereignty over the Paracel and Spratly Islands in the SCS. Vietnam may quibble that the Pham Van Dong letter did not create an agreement, much less a binding one. The answer to this quibble is that from the point of international law, well established through cases and repeated state practice, is that what makes a binding agreement is neither its form, nor its designation (i.e., name), but the indispensable element of commitment. The key word is "commitment." In the classical *Legal Status of Eastern Greenland* case (Demark v. Norway, 1933), the Permanent Court of International Justice (PCIJ) found Norway inescapably bound by an oral assurance made by its own Foreign Minister to Denmark, because it clearly transmitted a commitment, although given in oral form.[54] Besides, the concept of "apparent authority" (the decisive capacity for making a binding commitment for an agreement) in the law governing contract/treaty making, which the Norwegian Foreign Minister

---

[53] Vietnam, like China, is a party to the Convention. Full text of the Convention in 1155 U.N.T.S. 331 (1969).

[54] 1933 P.C.I.J. (series A/B), No. 53, p. 71.

possessed as his country's Foreign Minister (like that of the vice president for sales of a business company), would apply without fail to Prime Minister Pham Van Dong, as Vietnam's Prime Minister.

The final conclusion, from the above, is that Vietnam's reversion from its pre-1975 position failed to pass the test of international law, either customary law or treaty law.

The Philippines' Claim

The Philippines also claims the Spratly Islands based on the theory that they form part of the Philippine archipelago. Alternatively, it invoked the principle of *res nullius*, or abandoned territories since the end of World War II, when Japan exited the region; and under the SFPT, Japan simply "surrendered" the SCS islands it had occupied, but without naming a recipient-owner. It also mentioned its continental shelf extension as a basis of claim.[55]

In 1956, a Filipino named Tomas Clomas launched a private expedition to the Spratly Islands and claimed them, calling them "Freedomland." The ROC (Taiwan) government protested to the Manila government and stationed troops on Itu Aba (Taiping 太平島), the largest island in the Spratly Islands, with fresh water to sustain human life, in order to defend the island group. In 1968, however, the Philippine government publicly presented the same islands in Clomas' "Freedomland" as the Kalayaan (Freedom) Islands. Ten years later, in 1978, it formally claimed the Kalayaans by a Presidential decree.[56] The islands have since been administered as a part of Palawan Province.[57] Thus, the Philippines laid its claim to the islands they occupied. (The discussion of The Philippines v. China arbitration will appear in Chapter 4.)

---

[55] Valencia *et al.*, see note 8, 33f.

[56] "Presidential Decree No. 1596 — Declaring Certain Area Part of the Philippine Territory and Providing for Their Government and Administration," *Chan Robles Law Library*, June 11, 1978.

[57] *Fil-AM Bulletin* (Manila), March 5, 1974.

My evaluation of these Philippine bases of claim is twofold: (a) The *res nullius* claim is falsified by the fact that a devolution clause was inherent in the 1952 ROC–Japan bilateral treaty, as explained before. Besides, Toma Cloma's occupation of the "Freedomland" islands lasted only a few months. At the time Clomas staked out his claim, the Philippine government neither approved nor disapproved his actions and claim.[58] (b) The continental shelf claim also cannot stand up on its own, because the deep Palawan Trough separates the Spratly Islands from the Philippine archipelago; there is no "natural prolongation," as required by Art. 76 of the UNCLOS treaty, if the Philippines should attempt to extend its continental shelf claim beyond the 200 nautical miles limit up to an ultimate 350 nautical miles range.

Malaysia's Claim

Malaysia claims 12 islands and features of the SCS, and occupies six of them, including one island, Swallow Reef (Pulau Layang-Layang), and five reefs plus one shoal.[59] For these, it sets out two legal bases of claim, namely: continental shelf extension and the rule of discovery/ occupation. The first of these two legal bases of its claim arises out of the 1958 Convention on the Continental Shelf, which Malaysia signed in 1960. Malaysia passed its own Continental Shelf Act in 1966 and 1969, modeled after the 1958 treaty, defining the country's continental shelf as "the seabed and subsoil of submarine areas adjacent to the coast of Malaysia," up to 200m deep or the limit of exploitability. A related domestic law, the Petroleum Mining Act of 1966, governs the exploration and development of natural resources "both on- and offshore." A most explicit depiction of Malaysia's continental shelf claim is a map it published in 1979, entitled: "Map Showing the Territorial Waters and Continental Shelf Boundaries."[60]

[58] Valencia *et al.*, see note 8, p. 35.

[59] See the six names spelled out in a discussion in Valencia *et al.*, see note 8, p. 36. See also "Malaysia's Border Disputes," in Wikipedia, the free encyclopedia.

[60] Daniel J. Dzurek, "Boundary and Resource Disputes in the South China Sea,"

In this map, Malaysia defined its continental shelf area and claimed all the islands arising from it.[61]

Due to its geography, Malaysia is further removed from China, and has actually disputed more with Vietnam, Singapore, and the Philippines than with China, not to mention its dispute with Indonesia in the Celebes Sea, between the Indonesian Province of North Kalimantan and Federal Malaysia's Sabah state.[62]

Vietnam, which claims the entire Spratly group on historical grounds, and claims all islands/features occupied and claimed by Malaysia. Malaysia also has overlapping claims with the Philippines, over the continental shelf and islands in the Spratly Islands area. A small portion of the area of the overlapping claim by Malaysia and the Philippines is also claimed by Brunei.

Malaysia and Vietnam jointly submitted a notification in 2009 to the Commission on the Limits of the Continental Shelf (CLCS), under Art. 76 of the UNCLOS. The notification is about the two countries' extended continental shelf claims. In its wake, China lodged an objection with the U.N. Secretary General, complaining that the area claimed in the joint Vietnam–Malaysia submission was under Chinese sovereignty.[63] Another objection was received from the Philippines.[64] The joint Vietnam-Malaysia submission defined the area which both countries were jointly claiming, although it did not define the extended continental shelf that each claimed. The Philippine objection said that the defined area in the joint submission

---

Ocean Yearbook, vol. 5 (1985): 254, 282.

[61] Lee G. Cordner, "The Spratly Island Dispute and the Law of the Sea," *Ocean Development and International Law*, vol. 25 (1994): 64.

[62] The litigation between Malaysia and Indonesia, over the Ligitan and Sipadan islands, ended in a judgment by the International Court of Justice (ICJ) in 2002 that found in Malaysia's favor.

[63] Chinese Premier WEN Jiabao said all countries with territorial claims in the South China Sea should strictly follow the Declaration on the Code of Conduct in the South China Sea.

[64] See CLCS, "Outer limits of the continental shelf beyond 200 nautical miles from the baselines: Joint Submission by Malaysia and the Socialist Republic of Viet Nam," UN's Division for Ocean Affairs and the Law of the Sea.

was subject to a claim by the Philippines as well as subject to territorial disputes over "some of the islands in the area including North Borneo." The dispute raised by the Philippines remained unresolved at the time of this writing.

Malaysia also had a dispute with Singapore, over several islets at the eastern entrance to the Singapore Strait, namely: Pedra Branca (previously called Pulau Batgu puteh), Middle Rocks, and South Ledge. The suit was brought before the International Court of Justice (ICJ) in 2003, and the Court decided in a judgment handed down in 2008 that Pedra Branca belonged to Singapore, and Middle Rocks belonged to Malaysia.[65]

Malaysia seemed to be of two minds in dealing with China in its disputes over the SCS. On November 1, 2016, Najib Razak, the Malaysian leader, signed an agreement during a visit in Beijing which called for naval cooperation between the two countries, to "ensure peace and stability in the South China Sea." Najib said that while Malaysia would not compromise on its SCS claims, it would want them to be worked out through dialogue and peaceful negotiations, an approach always preferred by China. But just a little over one month later, on December 19, the same year, Malaysia was calling on the 10-nation Association of Southeast Asian Nations (ASEAN), of which it is a member, to support it in its dispute with China over the Southeast China Sea.[66]

Brunei's Claim

Brunei Darussalam (or "The Abode of Peace") gained independence from Britain in 1982. Its dispute with China began in 1984, when it adhered to the 1982 UNCLOS, and declared an EEZ of 200 nautical miles, which extends into part of the Spratly Island group. In contrast to the more vocal governments in Hanoi and Manila, Brunei is what

---

[65] *Judgement ICJ Report* 2008, 12ff.

[66] "Malaysia calls for Asean support against Beijing over South China Sea," retrieved March 14, 2017, www.todayonline.com/.../asia/malaysia-calls-asean-support-against-beijing-over-s-china sea

one analyst calls a "quiet claimant." And its claims are more associated with maritime jurisdiction than sovereignty.[67]

Brunei established diplomatic relations with China in 1991, but also maintains close relations with Great Britain, its former colonial ruler, and the United States. There has been limited news on its discussion over sovereignty issues with China since 1991. The most important stabilizing factor in Brunei–PRC relations is China's dependence on Brunei's vast, though declining, reserves in hydrocarbons (oil). Since 2014, the Brunei-Guangxi Economic Corridor led to over $500 million in joint investments to develop strategic industries by early 2016. More was expected to come as a result of Beijing's Maritime Silk Road initiative. Chinese company Zhejiang Hengyi Group already began constructing a new refinery in Brunei with a capacity of 148,000 barrels per day, and a scheduled completion date by 2009. Given these growing economic ties and resource dependency, plus the limited and quiet Brunei claims in the SCS area, it is unlikely that the tranquil waters of "Abode of Peace" will face untold disturbances anytime soon.[68]

Concluding Comments

This chapter has shown that, despite the heuristic value in comparing China's position vis-à-vis the SCS to the United States' position vis-à-vis the Caribbean, China's hold on the SCS is far less firm, compared with America's grip on the Caribbean. The challenge posed by the four other contesting States (Vietnam, the Philippines, Malaysia, and Brunei) is real, and mostly formidable, if we discount the ROC (Taiwan) for the reasons given earlier.

Critics, especially in the United States, have picked on China on many issues. But, one item we have not touched on, thus far, as it is not directly an issue of territorial claims, is the artificial island construction by China in the SCS. It has become such a fixation in attacks

---

[67] Gary Sands, "Brunei, Silent Claimant in the South China Sea," *Foreign Policy Association*, April 28, 2016.

[68] Ibid.

on real or alleged Chinese "assertiveness" that the new Secretary of State Rex Tillerson, during his Senate confirmation hearings, even aired a policy stance seeking to stop the Chinese island-building acts and, moreover, to block China's access to these artificial islands.[69] This access-denial theme ricocheted through wider corridors in America, among both government and media circles. Often, it was coupled with accusations of China's alleged denial of the freedom of navigation to foreign (American) ships in the SCS. The hidden irony is that, if indeed China's alleged denial of the freedom of navigation in the SCS can be empirically sustained — which China denied is true — how is it different from Tillerson's version of an American access denial to China, blocking it from these artificial islands in the SCS?

That said, the truth is that other than China, as one report reveals, several other countries, including Vietnam, the Philippines, Malaysia, and so on, have all constructed or expanded islands in the SCS, to fortify their claims to territory.[70] But, the reason why China commanded so much more attention than all the others is both the speed and the scale of the Chinese construction spree and, more important, the alarm it has raised to U.S. strategic interests. We shall return to this point in Chapter 5.

I hope to conclude this chapter by offering a further comment on the divergence between two methodologies in analyzing the complex SCS conflicts, namely: one is focused on islands as most extant discourses have done, and the other one, which is our preference, approaches the question from the perspective of historic waters, in terms of both its legal significance and practical utility for the quest of a reasonable resolution. Not to duplicate what has been said thus far or what will be discussed in later chapters, I would like to offer some

---

[69] John Glaser, "Tillerson's South China Sea Proposal Won't Work," *The Diplomat*, January 14, 2017.

[70] Alexandra Ma, "Here Is What You Need to Know about the South China Sea Disputes," *HUFPOST*, retrieved February 26, 2016, www.huffingtonpost.com/news/souh-china-sea-dispute. She cited a report with satellite images analyzed by Washington-based think tank Center for Strategic and International Studies (CSIS).

food for thought, on just the question of methodological comparison. It is about what the historic-waters approach (HWA, for short) can do, or will have the potential for, that the island-focused approach (IFA) cannot. I can think of four such points as a difference.

1. First, the IFA sees the disputes as mainly about who owns the islands. The rest of the SCS, in this perspective, is the body of waters surrounding the islands, including the territorial sea and the EEZ, plus the continental shelf that extends from each island. Hence, the solution to the disputes is to sort out who owns which island or island group. The HWA, on the other hand, views the SCS as an integral marine region, or a whole body of water which subsumes the islands, atolls, reefs, and other features within it. Thus, the solution to the tangling disputes lies in first determining which State owns the historic waters (let us assume State A); and the islands and the rest of the features, enclosed within the historic waters, accrue to that State or has a special relations with it under its historic title (State A).
2. Second, in the IFA discussions, an overwhelming attention is devoted to the islands, as opposed to the waters surrounding them; hence, not enough attention is given to the protection of the "collective goods," such as the fisheries (and other resources), in these waters. Issues like preservation of the fisheries and protection against overfishing are likely to escape equal attention of the analysts using the IFA method. Individual claimant States are likely to be less disposed to the problem of collective shared-resource management,[71] and measures designed to further its implementation. In the final analysis, collective shared-resource management may hold the key to an amicable resolution of the SCS disputes, a topic to which we will return in the concluding chapter below.
3. Third, so much wrangling has been heard, in the IFA analyses, over the question of the EEZ either in a claimant State's

[71] A good discussion of the question of shared-resource management is found in Valencia, see note 7, p. 59.

assertion (and defense) of its rights, or in a third-party assessment of a particular State's claim to an SCS island. The HWA, on the other hand, will show that such considerations, and verbiage, about the EEZ or, for that matter, any similar feature, will have a different meaning. The reason is that if the issue of historic waters is firmly established (i.e., who owns this body of historic waters), then the legal status of ownership of the islands, the EEZ, and other features will have to be teased out with who owns the historic waters in view.

4. Fourth, in view of the HWA's concerns, and the dictate of collective shared-resource management as a necessary measure for the ultimate resolution of the SCS disputes, the part of the general international law of territorial acquisition pertaining to the issue of historic waters may prove to be of particular value. By that, I am referring to its utility in the quest for a final solution that will be most equitable to the claimant States. In doing so, it will hold the key to the removal of the tensions that, if unmitigated, may have the potential of escalating to the level of Armageddon, especially with a U.S. superpower watching restlessly on the sidelines.

With that in view, we are ready to move on to a more systematic discourse on the topic and theory of historic waters in general international law, in the next chapter.

Chapter

3

"Historic Waters" in General International Law, and as Tested in Judicial Cases

On the subject of the law of the sea, most analysts, even many experts, look to the 1982 U.N. Convention on the Law of the Sea (UNCLOS III) as if it was the sole authoritative guide, to the neglect of norms in the broader general (customary) international law. It follows therefore that, as the 1982 Convention is totally silent on the question of "historic waters," almost all extant discussions on the South China Sea (SCS) disputes touched on all other legal issues, to the exclusion of historic waters, which is rooted in the Chinese claim over the SCS. This book is an attempt to fill the unfortunate gap; or, to put it more bluntly, to correct the common blunder. And this chapter is devoted to a full explication of the concept and theory of historic waters, in general international law (as opposed to, and much broader than, treaty law).

Most analysts apparently missed out on what the preamble of UNCLOS III admonishes, that "matters not regulated by this Convention continue to be governed by the rules and principles of *general international law*" (emphasis added). In fact, the support found in general international law for the concept of historic waters has a long history, and it has been upheld and expounded in a number of judicial cases.

The present discussion will duly place the concept of historic waters in the context of general (customary) international law, as the title of this chapter expressly indicates.

The topic itself, in fact, is not as obscure as one might assume. The U.S. Supreme Court, for example, has found the waters of the Mississippi Sound and Long Island Sound to be "historic" for purposes of disputes between the U.S. federal government and the coastal states (i.e., states in the American Union) regarding ownership of the seabed of the Sounds. The Supreme Court has also held that certain other bodies of U.S. waters do not meet the criteria for historic waters. These include Cook Inlet, Alaska; Santa Monica and San Pedro Bays, California; Florida Bay; numerous bays along the coast of Louisiana; Block Island Sound; and Nantucket Sound in Massachusetts.[1]

In a table showing "Claims Made to Historic Waters" in the world, prepared by the U.S. State Department's Bureau of Ocean Affairs, a number of states are listed as having either claimed a body of waters as "historic," or joined in an agreement with a neighboring country in designating a body of waters or a bay as "historic." These include, for example, Canada's Hudson Bay and Cambodia's 1982 historic waters agreement with Vietnam regarding a part of the Gulf of Thailand. The same State Department office has also produced a table of "excessive maritime claims," including "unrecognized historic-waters claims." To some of these cases, the United States has lodged protests, such as to the Soviet claim to Peter the Great Bay, Libya's claim to the Gulf of Sidra, Italy's Gulf of Tarato claim, among others. The United States has also protested to bilateral agreements

[1] U.S. Naval War College, "Historic Waters," retrieved http://www.edu/getatachmentg/cd1fb225-30b4-4cfe.../HISTORIC-WATERS.aspx.

laying claims to certain "historic waters," such as the Cambodia–Vietnam agreement named earlier, and the India–Sri Lanka agreement laying claims to the Gulf of Mannar and Palk Bay.[2] What is interesting for our purpose here is that China's name does not appear on either of the two lists.

The reason why China is not among the targets of U.S. protests is most likely attributable to the fact that, contrary to the allegations by some commentators, China never claims the entire SCS as its historic waters. As is amply explained in Chapter 2, China's claim, based on the U-shaped 9-dash line, is limited to the maritime area within the U-shaped region, resembling a cow's tongue. The landward space left between the U-shaped line itself and the putative coastlines of the other Littoral States encircling it, as can be seen in the map provided in Chapter 2, suggests a clear allowance for the territorial sea belonging to each of these other states surrounding the Chinese-drawn U-shaped line. Thus, the Chinese line is nonexclusionary.

The exclusion of China from the list of countries which the United States considers to be making "excessive claims" on historic waters is of extreme illustrative value, for the criteria supporting the legality of historic waters in general international law. The three such criteria are (a) the authority exercised over the area by the state claiming it as its "historic waters"; (b) the continuity (i.e., duration) of such exercise of authority; and (c) the attitude of foreign states.[3] These criteria are replicated in the measure employed by the U.S. State Department, although expressed in slightly different language. The third criterion in the U.S. measure is the "acquiescence," rather than the "attitude," of other states.[4] It thus makes sense why in

[2] U.S. Department of State, Bureau of Oceans, *Limits in the Sea*, No. 114: *U.S. Responses to Excessive Maritime Claims* (March 9, 1992), 7ff.

[3] As laid out in Document A/Cn.4/145: "Judicial Regime of Historic Waters Including Historic Bays — Study Prepared by the [ILC] Secretariat," p. 25; excerpted from *Yearbook of the U.N. International Law Commission* 1962, Vol. II.

[4] These same three criteria are iterated, for instance, in the U.S. protest to the claim made in Cambodia's agreement with Vietnam regarding part of the Gulf of Thailand dated July 7, 1982. U.S. Department of State, Bureau of Oceans, *Limits in the Sea*, p. 13.

America's attempt to restrain China in the SCS, the specific charge is nothing other than the threat that China poses to the freedom of navigation (RON), as we have seen thus far.[5] The absence (or infeasibility) of a U.S. protest to the Chinese historic waters claim in the SCS, which meets all the three identified criteria, leaves the RON the only legal ground on which the United States can lay a complaint at the Chinese doorstep. Unlike Libya under Qaddafi, which claimed all the 150,000 square miles of the Gulf of Sidra as "internal waters," China does not claim the entire SCS, nor does it claim the maritime area enclosed by the U-shaped line as its internal waters (see below). Hence, no duplicate of U.S. protest to Libya is warranted in regard to China.

The Concept, Definition, and Theory of Historic Waters

Concept

In a 1962 document pertaining to a study by the U.N. International Law Commission (ILC), the concept of "historic waters" is traced to its root in the practice of states through the ages whereby they claimed and maintained sovereignty over maritime areas, which they considered vital to them, without paying much attention to divergent and changing opinions about what international law might prescribe with respect to the delimitation of the territorial sea.[6] After acknowledging that a definition of the concept of historic waters is hardly possible for lack of a consensus among nations, the report lists two factors contributing to its rise over time. One was the "controversial

---

[5] Cf. Brookings Institution, Center for East Asian Studies, East Asia Policy Paper (Je. 2016): *The U.S. RON Program in the South China Sea: A Lawful and Necessary Response to China's Strategic Ambiguity.*

[6] Document A/CN.4/143, see n. 3 above.

Downloaded from the ILC website http://www.un.org/law/ilc/index.htm. However, some commentators traced the first claim of such historic title to the *U.S. in the North Atlantic Fisheries Arbitration* of 1910. For example, T. Scovazzi in D. Pharand and U. Leanza, *The Continental Shelf and Economic Zone: Delimitation of Legal Regime* (Kluwer, 1993), p. 322.

status of the international legal rules relating to the delimitation of the maritime territory of the State" (Para. 36). The other factor in the development of the concept and theory of historic waters was the "attempts, official and unofficial, to substitute for the controversial and doubtful international law relating to the delimitation of territorial waters a set of clear-cut, generally acceptable, written rules on the subject" (Para. 37).

The report, which is appropriately titled "Juridical Regime of Historic Waters, Including Historic Bays," cites the position by an eminent authority on the subject, Sir Gerald Fitzmaurice, a former judge of the International Court of Justice (ICJ) who states in an article with reference to the *Fisheries* case (U.K. v. Norway, 1951):

> "The Norwegian contention was essentially an attempt to remove from the conception of 'historicity' of given rights, the element of prescription, that is, in effect, the element of an adverse acquisition of rights in the face of existing law. Yet, this element is of the essence of the matter, for a title or right based on historical considerations only becomes material when (and indeed assumes that) the actions involved are not or could not be justified according to the recognized rules, and can therefore be justified, if at all, only by reference to some special factor such as an *historic right.*
>
> "As was suggested in the United Kingdom's written reply in the *Fisheries* case, this right takes the form essentially of a 'validation in the international legal order of a usage which is intrinsically invalid', by the continuance of the usage over a *long period of time*"[7] (Para. 43) (emphasis added).

The same UN ILC document then named a few other authors who considered the juridical regime of "historic waters" in the same vein as did Sir Gerald Fitzmaurice. They included: Westlake, Fauchille, Pitt-Corbett, Higgins and Colombos, Balladore Pallieri, among others. Pertinent quotations from their works are found in the U.N. Secretariat memorandum on "historic bays" (A/CONF, 13.1), pp. 18–20.

[7] *British Year Book of International Law*, vol. 30 (1953): pp. 27–28.

Theory

The theory of historic waters is exemplified in the *Fisheries* case (1951), as argued by the United Kingdom and affirmed in the final decision by the ICJ. It is based on the premise that a state can only establish a title to areas of sea . . . on the basis of a historic or prescriptive title.[8] The two essential elements in such a historic or prescriptive title are: (a) actual exercise of authority by the claimant state and (b) acquiescence by other states.[9]

Definition

Despite the difficulty acknowledged in the UN ILC document about the definition of a "historic waters" claim for lack of a consensus among nations, one commentator did offer a workable definition in his study of the legal regime of historic bays (applicable to historic waters) in international law, which has been widely accepted, as follows:

> Waters over which the Coastal State, contrary to the generally applicable rules of international law, clearly, effectively, continuously, and over a substantial period of time, exercise sovereignty rights with the acquiescence of the community of States.[10]

For clarity, I must hasten to add that although in this definition, historic waters are established "contrary to the applicable rules of international law" at a given time, the title, once established, is protected by general international law. Establishment of a right and maintenance of an established right are to be differentiated. The earlier definition is intrinsically based on what is affirmed in the *Fisheries* case, and as clarified by Sir Gerald Fitzmaurice.

---

[8] ICJ, Proceedings, Oral Arguments, Documents, Fisheries Case, vol. II, p. 302.
[9] Ibid., p. 303.
[10] L. H. Bouchez, *The Regime of Bays in International Law* (The Hague: Martinus Nijhoff, 1964), p. 281.

Historic Waters in General International Law as Tested in ICJ Cases

The ICJ had occasion to hear two cases in which it affirmed the legitimacy of titles to "historic waters." The first one is the *Fisheries* case (1951) the importance of which, to reiterate, is that the Court rejected the British view that Norway's claim of historic waters was contrary to international law. The moral is that historic waters is protected by general international law, once established.

In the Case Concerning the Continental Shelf (Tunisia v. Libya, 1982), the court acknowledged the existence of "historic waters," but noted that general international law does not provide for a *single* 'regime' for 'historic waters' or 'historic bays,' but only for a particular regime for each of the concrete, recognized cases of 'historic waters' or 'historic bays'."

Other than China, a few states such as Russia, Norway, Libya, Canada, and Tonga also claim their own historic waters.

Historic Waters and Historic Rights Differentiated

In his phenomenal work on the subject,[11] Clive R. Symmons points out that historic waters should not be confused with "historic rights," which is different in meaning. A claim based on the latter differs in two ways. First, a claim of historic rights only applies on a *quoad hunc* basis, not *erga omnes*, as does a claim of historic waters. Second, historic rights do not amount to zonal claims of jurisdiction or sovereignty. As Judge De Castro stated in the *Fisheries Jurisdiction* cases (not to be confused with the 1951 Fisheries case),[12] historic rights of states concerned with "high seas fishing," for instance, do not give them "acquisition over the sea by prescription," but merely "respected" rights by "long usage."

---

[11] Clive R. Symmons, *Historic Waters in the Law of the Sea: A Modern Re-Appraisal* (The Hague: Martinus Nijhoff, 2008), pp. 4–6.
[12] [1974] ICJ Rep. 3, p. 99.

The Legal Status of the Waters Enclosed by the U-Shaped Line

Let us connect the dots, by raising a number of questions, beginning with the following first question:

1. Does the maritime area enclosed within the Chinese-drawn U-shaped line meet the standards for the delimitation of "historic waters"?

Answer: As we have seen from the facts presented in the preceding two chapters, the Chinese claim based on the U-shaped line meets all the three criteria in the international law governing "historic waters," to wit:

a. The exercise of Chinese authority over the maritime area — actually began since the 3rd century BC, such as through the functioning of three prefectural authorities, dispatch of troops to patrol the area, etc.
b. Continuity of this exercise of authorities — has been uninterrupted since then all the way through the present. The three prefectural governments have come down to be replaced by the governance structure anchored in the Province of Hainan Island.
c. The acquiescence of foreign states — is shown, *inter alia*, by the exclusion of China from the abovementioned list of countries making "excessive maritime claims" that elicited U.S. protests. Moreover, when the 1947 Chinese map announcing the U-shaped 11-dash line (later reduced to 9-dash line) was publicly announced, it received no objection or protest from any country or territory (e.g., colonies).
d. As shown before, it was readily incorporated into a Rand-McNally map of the same year. Whatever dissent was heard later came only after the 1950s. The legality of the Chinese claim was supported by the "contemporaneous" international law of 1947.

2. A second legal question that can be raised is: Since the 1947 map was drawn and announced by the pre-Communist Republic of China

(ROC) government, how is all this related to the People's Republic of China (PRC), which did not come into being until the Communist Party won the civil war, two years later, in 1949? The question is even more complicated as the ROC, now relocated in Taiwan, continues to cling to its claim over the SCS based on the U-shaped line that it drew in 1947 when its government was seated in Nanjing (Nanking), on the mainland. Does this impinge upon the PRC's claim to the SCS?

Answer: The PRC purports to be the successor to the state of China that was represented, at the time when the U-shaped line was promulgated, by the ROC under the pre-Communist government of Chiang Kai-shek, whose credentials were then accepted as the representative of the State of China by the international community at large. The PRC considers the current division across the Taiwan Strait as a transient situation, pending the final reunification of the two sides. The present division is clearly acknowledged by the international community, as 174 of the world's states (plus Palestine) accord their diplomatic recognition to the PRC, and 21 others continue to recognize ROC/Taiwan. As we noted before, the two Chinese regimes have identical claims to the SCS on the basis of historic waters, as defined, and confined, by the U-shaped 9-dash line. Theoretically, if any disagreement should occur between them, it would be like a "domestic" dispute between the two Chinese regimes, seated as they are, respectively, in Taipei and Beijing. But, at the pragmatic level, the two sides seem to follow a de facto policy of mutual tolerance. Taipei, for example, maintains troops on Ito Abba (太平島, Taiping Island), the largest in the Nansha (Spratly) Island group; and Beijing has constructed artificial islands out of islets and reefs in the SCS. Neither has elicited opposition from the other side. As noted elsewhere, ROC/Taiwan has elected to co-opt the new nomenclature of the U-shaped line, calling it the "9-dash line," instead of the original "11-dash line," after the post–1949 PRC government removed two dashes from the original U-shaped line. Thus, ROC/Taiwan is implicitly, by sufferance, giving its acquiescence to the PRC's share in the State of China's claim to the historic waters in the SCS enclosed by the U-shaped line.

3. Still another question is the exact legal status of the waters encircled within the U-shaped line. In other words, is this body of "historic waters" analogous to internal waters, or not?

In its Section E "Legal Status of the Waters Regarded as 'Historic Waters'," the same UN ILC document raised the same question; and in an inconclusive answer it merely suggested a distinction between the analogies of internal waters and territorial waters. The end difference is that if historic waters are like territorial waters, then the Littoral State "must allow innocent passage of foreign ships," under the modern law of the sea. But it "has no such obligations with respect to internal waters."[13]

Neither the ROC nor the PRC has offered any definitive characterization of the legal status of the waters encircled by the U-shaped line, as to whether they are "internal waters." As has been pointed out in one study, opinions within the ROC government were divided on this point. One consideration weighing against the "internal waters" view was the fact that the ROC government never tried to stop foreign ships, including warships, from navigating through the waters enclosed by the U-shaped line after its promulgation since 1948.[14]

That being the case, one speculation why PRC has chosen not to characterize the waters encircled by the U-shaped line as internal waters is that it may have resulted from a hidden popularity contest with the ROC. Beijing just does not want to play the "bad guy" denying innocent passage of foreign vessels by declaring these waters as internal waters.[15] If this is true, then when faced with the United States' anxiousness to stigmatize it for denying the freedom of navigation to foreign ships in the SCS, Beijing may find no reason to attach an internal waters label to the maritime area encircled within the U-shaped line.

That said, it is necessary, however, to note that in 1992, the National People's Congress (NPC), the Chinese legislature, adopted

---

[13] Document A/CN.4/143, see note 6, p. 23.

[14] Yann-huei Song and Peter Kien-hong Yu, "China's 'Historic Waters' in the South China Sea: An Analysis from Taiwan, ROC," *American Asian Review*, vol. 12, no. 4 (1994): pp. 83–101, 92.

[15] Ibid., p. 94.

the "Law on the Territorial Sea and the Contiguous Zone of the PRC." By this Law, the PRC's baseline for delimiting the territorial sea is determined by the method of straight baselines, formed by joining the various base points (headlands) with straight lines — not following the curvatures of the zigs and zags of the coastlines.[16] The method, which closely resembles the provision in Art. 7 of UNCLOS III, applies equally to the major SCS islands claimed by China, including the Paracel and Spratly islands.

According to UNCLOS III, waters on the landward side of the baseline are part of the internal waters of the Littoral State. Thus, a large part of the waters off China's coasts and those off the islands claimed by China in the SCS will become China's internal waters, subject to its sovereignty, if Beijing chooses to enforce the 1992 Law in conformity with the UNCLOS III's definition of the territorial sea. Except for innocent passage of their ships, other states will enjoy no rights in these Chinese internal waters. Moreover, areas up to 24 and 200 miles (nm) measured from the baselines will, respectively, become China's contiguous zone and EEZ. In such a case, the total of the combined maritime areas subject to China's sovereignty and jurisdiction will be enlarged to such an extent that it may even exceed the size of the "historic waters" enclosed by the U-shaped line, according to estimates in one study.[17]

In conclusion, this 1992 domestic law adopted by the Chinese NPC further complicates the problems in the SCS disputes already inflamed by the "historic waters" variable highlighted by the U-shaped 9-dash line beginning with China's 1947 map.

Countering Third-Party Challenges to the Legality of the Chinese Claim

Due cognizance should be made of serious third-party critiques of the Chinese claim based on the U-shaped 9-dash line. By "third parties" we mean quarters other than the competing claimant states regarding

[16] Song and Yu, see note 14, p. 94.

[17] Ibid.

the SCS. In particular, two of them deserve to be singled out for priority consideration: one by the U.S. State Department (2014) and the other contained in an article published in the prestigious *American Journal of International Law* (AJIL) in 2013. We begin with the latter article.

The article: "Legal Analysis of China's Historic Rights Claim in the South China Sea" (AJIL).[18] It was written by two distinguished coauthors: Florian Dupuy, an Associate at LALIVE, a Swiss firm specializing in international legal matters, and Pierre-Marie Dupuy, Professor of International Law at the University of Paris. The coauthors turned their perspicacious sight on what they termed as a "striking contrast" (read: contradiction) between "China's assertive stance and far-reaching pretensions in the South China Sea," on the one hand, and "the indeterminacy of its legal position by the deliberative use of ambiguous terminology and tacit reliance on principles not recognized by international law," on the other. Their conclusion, as can be expected, is: "China's assertiveness and its reiteration of indeterminate claims do not constitute, from a legal perspective, a position that is even minimally persuasive."[19]

With due respect, my considered overall comment is that the coauthors applied too rigid a legal perspective — tinged with the gross self-confidence imbued with a peculiar culture-borne sense of justice (righteousness) — and unconscionably held China responsible solely to the provisions set by the UNCLOS III, despite the convention's total silence on the question of historic waters. Obviously, the coauthors did not see any "striking contrast" in this deliberate or haphazard mismatch, between a claim based on "historic waters," on the one hand, and the UNCLOS III, on the other.

Before going into the specifics, let us consider the coauthors' criticism of China's "deliberative use of ambiguous terminology and tacit reliance on principles *not recognized by international law*"

[18] Florian Dupuy and Pierre-Marie Dupuy, "Legal Analysis of China's Historic Rights in the South China Sea," *American Journal of International Law*, vol. 107, no. 1 (January 2013): pp. 124–141.

[19] Ibid., p. 140.

(emphasis added). My reaction is twofold. One, to the extent that the coauthors use UNCLOS III as the gauge of what they believe is the "international law" relevant to topics of the sea. It is no wonder, therefore, that the principles China relied on were those not recognized by this peculiar brand of "international law" known to the coauthors. Second, let us recall that an important element in the theory of historic waters, as crystallized and affirmed by the ICJ in the *Fisheries* case (1951), is that "a State can only establish a title to areas of sea *which do not come within these general rules of international law* on the basis of an historic or prescriptive title" (emphasis added).[20] That being so, why would the coauthors expect China to be different? In the article, the coauthors meticulously enumerated the various statements China made in asserting its claims regarding the SCS, from (a) the 1958 declaration made by Premier Zhou Enlai (Chou En-lai), on the breadth of China's territorial sea, which rule extended as well to the four named major groups of the SCS islands (Paracels, Spratlys, Pratas, and Mcclesfield Bank); (b) the Chinese "Law on the Territorial Sea and the Contiguous Zone," promulgated in 1992; (c) the 1996 statement accompanying China's ratification of the UNCLOS III, which also repeated China's claim to the same four major groups of SCS islands; (d) the two *notes verbales* filed in 2009 to the U.N. Secretary General by the PRC Permanent Mission to the United Nations; to (e) the one additional *note verbale* filed in 2011, following the submissions by Malaysia and Vietnam to the U.N. Commission on the Limit of the Continental Shelf (CLCS), when China reaffirmed its territorial claims over the four named major SCS island groups and the adjacent waters.

Despite all these documents, the coauthors complained that "the overall geographical scope of China's maritime claim remains unclear." They added a conclusive remark: "To our knowledge, the basis for China's broad sovereignty claim in the South China Sea has

---

[20] ICJ, Pleadings, Oral Arguments, Documents, Fisheries case, vol. II, p. 302; also as reproduced in UN ILC Document A/CN.4/143, Judicial Regime of Historic Waters, etc., see note 6, p. 8.

never been officially set out in clear legal terms."[21] This is very surprising, because even a casual reader would have noticed that the multiple documents enumerated by the coauthors repetitively identified China's claim to the four major island groups (the Paracels, Spratlys, Pratas, and Mcclesfield Bank) *plus* their adjacent waters. The simultaneous mention of "adjacent waters" is a unique feature in the Chinese assertion of claim. On top of this repetitive naming of the island groups and the adjacent waters, the Chinese statements often emphasized China's *historical* exercise of authority over the SCS, and produced the 1947 map to show what the Chinese claim covers within the U-shape line, as we have noted in all the first three chapters of this book, including this one. Concededly, the Chinese erred on the side of using peculiar Chinese terms like "authority" and "control," for example, rather than "sovereignty" and "jurisdiction," or terms understood as of "legal" significance to a lawyer steeped in Western international law.

The article then assailed the Chinese "sort of entitlement based on history" by picking on the different translations in secondary literature that came to the coauthors' attention. They found, for example, varied references to "historic rights" and "historical rights" in the Chinese claim. If the coauthors, however, were proficient in the Chinese language, they would readily know that the Chinese term lishi quanli (歷史權利) could translate as either "historic rights" or "historical rights," depending on the context and the preferences of the translators.

More or less the same cavalier attitude is shown in the coauthors' treatment of the *maps* that the Chinese took pains, time and again, to put forward, while expressing their claim to the SCS based on the element of historicity and acquisition by peaceful prescription over 23 centuries (beginning from the 3rd century BC). As the coauthors correctly pontificated, "maps do not constitute titles in international law." To prove their point, they cited judicial cases, such as the famous *Frontier Dispute* (Burkina Faso v. Republic of Mali, 1986), in which the ICJ ruled that in frontier delimitations "maps merely

[21] Ibid., p. 19.

constitute information." Exactly, what the Chinese maps do is to provide information, but, through so doing, to demonstrate the extent of the Chinese exercise of authority (which translates as sovereignty) since the time of antiquity and also its continuity throughout prolonged history. These facts were amply provided, so were the legal arguments propounded, in official documents[22] as well as in the sources cited in Chapter 2 of this book. It is strange that all these official documents and the sources we cited in that chapter escaped the attention of the coauthors who wrote the highly professional, but one-sided, article.

I would add one more point on the value and legal significance of the map showing the U-shaped line. The 1947 map was not made by just any casual cartographer, but by the Chinese government. As such, it was the final fruit of the toil of a high-powered committee of experts, after conducting a detailed review of the hard facts that took in view earlier maps which graphically reflected China's effective control of the maritime region in the SCS, as enforced by three prefectural governments and the patrol by government troops, from ancient through modern times.[23] Hence, when the 1947 map was publicly promulgated in January 1948 by the Chinese Government, it was much more than just the release of a piece of cartographic work. In and of itself, the map was an assertion of China's official claim to the SCS, the map serving as an illustration of the extent of Chinese authority (read: sovereignty) over it. No detailed description by words can do what the map does, on the precise extent and seriousness of the Chinese claim. It is perplexing that the coauthors who accuse the Chinese of "indeterminacy" and "unclear" fuzziness in their claim should try so hard to brush aside the detailed 1947 map as valueless. It is like blowing hot and cold in a legal game play.

Similarly, while they discounted the map as irrelevant, the coauthors then assailed the map for not being precise enough, for lack of geographical coordinates. If the Chinese cartographer were equally

---

[22] One example is "China's Indisputable Sovereignty over the Xisha and Nansha Islands," Document of the PRC Foreign Ministry (1980).

[23] Song and Yu, see note 14, esp. pp. 85–87.

cynical, he might have retorted with: "Why should the coordinates matter, if maps have so little value?"

What the coauthors probably intended to be a *coup de grace* was what they termed as the "repeated displays of disagreement by the States in the region."[24] They were referring to Vietnam and the Philippines, whose disagreements were aired, as the coauthors admitted, only after 1956. But, as all competent international lawyers know, according to the doctrine of "inter-temporal law," crystallized in the classic *Island of Palmas* case (U.S. v. Netherlands, 1928), and applied by ICJ in *Land and Maritime Boundary* (Cameroon v. Nigeria, 2002), a judicial act (incl. the enunciation of a right) must be "appreciated" (adjudged) by the contemporaneous international law, not by the subsequent (changed) law at the time of dispute. Hence, the historic title graphically expressed in 1947 for China should be adjudged by the prevailing international law at the time. Besides, the lack of protest and dissent by states and territories in the region at the time implied the prevalence of the necessary third element, *acquiescence* of other states, in the affirmation of China's historic title. The other two criteria for the affirmation of a historic title (such as over "historic waters") — (a) exercise of authority and (b) continuity of such exercise of authority — were all fulfilled in the Chinese case, as demonstrated in the historical facts presented in Chapter 2. Hence, the disagreements by Vietnam and the Philippines aired only after the 1950s would be ruled immaterial, under the doctrine of intertemporal law.

The second critique: The U.S. Department of State's analysis of China's 9-dash line.[25] This document prepared by the State Department's Bureau of Oceans was released on December 5, 2014, as a commentary on the two Chinese Notes Verbales submitted to the U.N. Secretary General for dissemination to U.N. member states.

---

[24] Dupuy and Dupuy, see note 18, p. 140.

[25] U.S. Department of State, Bureau of Oceans, Limits in the Seas, No. 143. China: Maritime Claims to the South China Sea, retrieved http://www/state/gov/e/oes/cons/opa/cl6065.htm.

The U.S. State Department study tests three possible interpretations of the Chinese dash-line claim as presenting, respectively, (a) a title to the islands the line encloses; (b) a national maritime boundary; and (c) a historically based claim to the waters that are exclusive to China (i.e., historic waters). Instead of commenting on the details of the study, which has been done eloquently by Sourabh Gupta,[26] I wish to look at the basic premise of the State Department's "analysis." This can be seen from its concluding line, that unless China can justify its claim "in accordance with the international law of the sea, as reflected in the LOS Convention, its dashed-line claim does not accord with the international law of the sea."[27] Thus, the study's basic premise rests on the conviction that the "international law of the sea" is coterminous with the LOS Convention, that is, the UNCLOS III, which is totally silent on the issue of "historic waters." Throughout its 24 pages of analysis, the State Department's study meticulously tested various aspects of China's claim based on the dashed line against the provisions, or lack of them, in the LOS Convention. The conclusion that China's claim "does not accord with the international law of the sea" is anticipated by the premise that international law of the sea is nothing other than the LOS Convention. Such reasoning, nevertheless, duplicates the trajectory of thinking displayed not only by the two coauthors of the article examined earlier, but also of most other critiques of China's claim. The Hague Arbitral Tribunal, in the arbitration between the *Philippines and China*, followed exactly the same logic of reasoning, as we see in Chapter 4.

Worse still is one argument in the State Department's study that the advent of exclusive LOS-based jurisdiction has overridden prior usage rights (based on historicity). The study noted that the LOS Convention's provisions relating to the EEZ, continental shelf, and high seas, "do not contain exceptions for historic claims," adding that "the Convention's provisions *prevail over any assertion of historic claims* made in those areas" (emphasis added). In support of this

---

[26] Sourabh Gupta, "Why U.S. Analysis of China's Nine-Dash Line Is Flawed," *East Asia Forum*, January 11, 2015.

[27] Ibid., see note 24, p. 24.

exclusionary view, the study then went on to cite the ICJ's 1984 judgment in the *Gulf of Maine* case.[28] In this connection, it must be pointed out that all this argument merely shows either a tragic ignorance or a willful neglect of the history in the development of modern law of the sea. As the U.N. Document "Juridical Regime of Historic Waters, Including Historic Bays" noted, the Second Committee at the Hague Codification Conference in 1930 set the tone of what was the forthcoming law, when it took the position in its report that the proposed codification of the rules of international law regarding territorial waters should not affect the historic rights which states might possess over certain parts of their coastal sea. As per its Articles 7 and 12, the 1958 Law of the Sea Convention shows that the Geneva Conference that produced the convention took the same position regarding historic rights.[29] The dictum, thus set, is that no subsequently emergent rules of international law of the sea will override, or vitiate the sanctity of titles and rights established by historicity.

Besides, the *Gulf of Mane* is a case concerning fishing rights only. In making a distinction between "historic rights" and "historic waters," Clive R. Symmons commented that "historic rights of States concerned with 'high sea fishing' do not give them 'acquisition over the sea by prescription'."[30] Hence, the intended analogy to China's broader historic waters claim is not relevant. On this point, Sourabh Gupta added a cogent comment that tribunal panels constituted subsequent to the *Gulf of Maine* decision, such as *Jan Mayen*, *Eritrea/Yemen*, *Qata/Bahrain*, *Barbados/Trinida and Tobago*, "have all backed the reading that such longstanding traditions [as China's] are entitled to the respect and protection of international law."[31]

One point made by the State Department document echoes, in general, a remark made by the two coauthors in the AJIL article

---

[28] Ibid., 20.

[29] U.N. Document A/CN.4/143, see note 3, Para. 72.

[30] Symmons, see note 11, at 5.

[31] Zourabh Gupta, "PacNet #88 — Testing China's — and the State Department's — Nine-Dash Line Claims," Center for Strategic and International Studies (CSIS), December 15, 2014, p. 4.

mentioned earlier, only in more precise terms, to wit: That the Chinese government has never published a law or decree giving the 9-dash line any domestic legal significance. Unfortunately, this is true, up to a point. So, as Gupta put it, "the onus is on China to explicitly declare an international law-compliant basis for its alignment of the nine-dash line."[32] It is hard not to agree, unless Beijing prefers a policy of "strategic ambiguity," for its own reasons.

I would add in agreement, nevertheless, that, rather than trying to convert the rest of the world to be conversant in the Chinese language, or even to accept agnosticism, it will be easier for China to learn to convey its thoughts on their historic-titles claim by using international law-compliant language. For better presenting the case concerning its historic claims — like "historic waters" — in the SCS, it might just as well be the least costly price that China needs to pay.

[32] Ibid.

Chapter

4

The PCA Arbitration between the Philippines and China: A Critique from General International Law

Rectification of Names

The arbitration involving the Philippines and China (2013–2016) is often referred to in the media, even among some analysts, as being heard by a "U.N. Arbitration Court."[1] The truth is that the United Nations itself was not involved in the least. The only reason why the "U.N." is mentioned is that the arbitral tribunal was constituted under Annex VII to a U.N. Convention, that is, the UNCLOS III. However, that did not make the tribunal a U.N. forum. The case, like all other arbitration cases, came before an arbitral "tribunal," not a "Court." In arbitration cases, what comes out of an arbitral tribunal

[1] For example, "UN Arbitration Court Rules against Beijing in South China Sea Dispute," *VOA News*, July 12, 2016.

is an "award," not a judgment, which can only be handed down by a real court like the International Court of Justice (ICJ). A vital difference between the two is that an arbitral tribunal is constituted on an *ad hoc* basis, whereas the ICJ is a standing institution with a fixed complement of 15 judges, elected to serve nine-year renewable terms.[2] And, in another difference, the rules of law and principles to be applied by an arbitral tribunal is to be decided *ad hoc* by an agreement, known as *compromis d'arbitrage*, between the disputant parties in a given case. But the ICJ, on the other hand, applies general international law (including customary and treaty norms), unless it chooses to decide *ex aequo et bono*, if the parties so agree.[3] Still another difference in an arbitration case is that the parties are not strictly considered in plaintiff-defendant terms, like in a judicial case decided by a court like the ICJ. Hence, the arbitration, in the correct terminology, was between "The Philippines *and* China," although the "Philippines v. China" variation is occasionally used for convenience.

The arbitral tribunal in this case was constituted in accordance with Article 3 of Annex 7 ("Arbitration") of the LOS Convention, which follows a format first set for the Permanent Court of Arbitration (PCA), established by the 1899 Hague Conference on the Pacific Settlement of International Disputes, a format that has become a model for all future arbitral tribunals.[4] Despite its name, the PCA is not a court, much less a permanent one, but provides a format and procedures for arbitration. It has, nevertheless, a permanent secretariat seated in The Hague, which serves as the Registry for arbitration cases. Although Annex 7 of UNCLOS III provides for its own procedures for the constitution of an arbitral tribunal when needed, it in essence mimics the PCA model, and it makes use of the PCA Registry. Hence, the *Philippines and China* case has an official designation of "PCA

[2] The ICJ judges are elected by the U.N. General Assembly and Security Council, under Art. 4 of the ICJ Statute.

[3] As per Art. 38(2) of the Statute of the International Court of Justice.

[4] For a description of how the PCA format has served as a model for the constitution of all subsequent arbitral tribunals, see James C. Hsiung, *Anarchy and Order: The Interplay of Politics and Law in International Relations* (Boulder, CO: Lynne Rienner, 1997), p. 75.

Case No. 2013–19," and it lists the PCA Registry as well. All preliminary information was channeled through the PCA website bureau@pca-cpa.org. Further information pertaining to Rules of Procedure, press releases, transcripts, and photographs of the hearings, the Award on Jurisdiction and Admissibility, and the final Award on Merits may be found at http://www.pca.com/web/view/u. Both are PCA websites. Thus, the case should be properly called a PCA arbitration case, not a "U.N. arbitration" nor "Hague arbitration" case, as is often billed in media reports. Since the PCA's official description is that it is not a part of the United Nations, to call *Philippines and China* a "U.N. arbitration case" is misleading, if not sacrilegious at that.

The Background of the Case: Genesis of China's Nemesis

In conformity with Art. 1 of Annex VII of UNCLOS III, the Philippines on January 22, 2013 formally addressed a *note verbale* (written notification) to the People's Republic of China (PRC), concerning the initiation of compulsory arbitration as per Art. 287 and Annex VII of UNCLOS III. Attached to the notification was a statement of claim "with respect to the dispute with China over the maritime jurisdiction of the Philippines in the West Philippine Sea." The latter reference is the new Philippine name for the South China Sea (SCS). Through its Embassy in Manila, on January 23, the Chinese Government rejected and returned the Philippines' notification, together with its attachment. It spurned the Tribunal's jurisdiction, vouching it would not participate in the proceedings, nor accept its findings. Later, Beijing elaborated on the reasons why China did not accept the Tribunal's jurisdiction, when it issued a full-fledged Position Paper addressed to the Tribunal, on December 7, 2014.[5]

Although not anticipated, China's absence and refusal to participate turned out to be a windfall of blessings for the Philippines, because the latter could then single-handedly influence the selection of the arbitrators, without any Chinese input. Under Art. 1(b,c,d) of

[5] "China's Position Paper," retrieved, www.fmprc.gov.cn/mfa_eng/zxxx_662805/t1217147.shtml.

Annex 7, relating to the procedure for the selection of the five arbitrators, China and the Philippines should each pick one arbitrator; and they together would choose the remaining three arbitrators by agreement. In the event should they not be able to agree, then under Art. 1(e), the President of the International Tribunal for the Law of the Sea (ITLOS) would "make the necessary appointments." But, in the absence of the nonparticipating China, the Philippines' unilateral preferences carried the day. And the office of the ITLOS President, who would be empowered by Art. 1(e) to play a role, happened to be occupied by a Japanese jurist, named Shunji Yanai, for 2011–2014 — not known as a friend of China's.

Furthermore, the rules of law and principles to be applied by the Arbitral Tribunal, which would have been spelled out in the required *compromis d'arbitrage,* were, in the absence of China, specified by the Philippines alone. Hence, the UNCLOS, which was the Philippines' preference, was the only law that the Tribunal applied in arriving at its rulings.

Inevitably, the understandable displeasure of the Arbitrators, over China's defiance and challenge to the Arbitral Tribunal's jurisdiction, would be another plus for the compliant Philippines in the dispute. The Tribunal considered but rejected the argument in the Chinese Position Paper that the Parties' dispute was actually about the delimitation of a maritime boundary between the two countries and therefore excluded from the Tribunal's jurisdiction through a declaration China made in 2006. On the contrary, the Tribunal held that each of the 15 Submissions by the Philippines reflected disputes between the two States concerning the interpretation or application of the Convention, although without the benefit of China's prior consent.

In its application, the Philippines asked the Tribunal to rule on three interrelated matters: (a) the source of the Parties' rights and obligations in the SCS, including the 9-dash line; (b) the status of certain maritime features claimed by both the Philippines and China; whether they were properly characterized as islands, rocks, low-tide elevations, or submerged banks under the UNCLOS III; and (c) whether certain Chinese activities in the SCS violated the same Convention, by interfering with the exercise of the Philippines' sovereign rights and freedoms under the Convention or through construction and fishing activities that had harmed the marine environment.

With the selection of UNCLOS III to be the law by which to exclusively determine China's rights, the case was irreversibly stacked against China from the very beginning, simply because the Convention has nothing to say on the question of "historic waters," the main basis of the Chinese claim in regard to the 9-dash line in the SCS. To be true, the Convention does address "historic bays," "historic title," and "historic objects," but nothing that is even remotely or indirectly linkable to "historic waters." As was shown in Chapter 3 of this book, a State's rights over "historic waters" were established by (a) exercise of sovereignty over the waters, (b) continuity over a prolonged period in the exercise of sovereignty, and (c) the acquiescence of the international community, including the support of the "contemporaneous" international law, at the time when the rights were first expressly asserted.

In its 15 Submissions to the Tribunal, the Philippines skillfully raised rhetorical questions which were phrased in such a way that the answers would come only after testing the matters concerned against the UNCLOS III. One notorious example was its first Submission, which asked the Tribunal to find that "China's maritime entitlements in the SCS, like those of the Philippines, may not extend beyond those permitted by the U.N. Convention on the Law of the Sea." The Tribunal's ruling on this rhetorical question could be easily foretold, that it would be totally unrelated to the historic-waters issue.

The Tribunal's Initial Award: Jurisdiction and Admissibility

If anyone should have assumed that China's denial of the tribunal's jurisdiction and refusal to participate in the proceedings would have *ipso facto* torpedoed the case, he could not have been any more wrong. Not only does Art. 9 of Annex VII provide for a "default of appearance" procedure, under which a party's refusal to attend "shall not constitute a bar to proceedings." The Tribunal, which was required by the same Art. 9, to "satisfy itself . . . that it has jurisdiction over the dispute," thus earnestly invited China to file its reactions to the matters raised by the Philippines. When China finally responded with a Position Paper, the Tribunal seized upon the document "as effectively constituting a plea concerning [accepting] the Tribunal's jurisdiction."[6] The Tribunal convened a Hearing on Jurisdiction and Admissibility that took place in The Hague on 7, 8, and 13 July 2015.

Considering that the Philippines initiated the case in January 2013, the Tribunal waited over two and a half long years before convening its hearings on Jurisdiction and Admissibility, it is apparent that the Tribunal was vacillating, during the interim, about the legitimacy of its own jurisdiction. What tipped the balance may just as well be the filing on December 7, 2014 of the Chinese Position Paper, as was duly admitted in the October 29, 2015 Press Release and the final Award of the Tribunal.[7]

After it completed its Hearing on Jurisdiction and Admissibility, the Tribunal announced its unanimous conclusion that it had jurisdiction to consider the Philippines' "claims" (i.e., requests for the Tribunal's rulings in its application) and whether these claims were admissible. While the Hearing during the first phase did not concern the "merits" of the case, which would come during the second phase, it was almost certain that the announcement as such already anticipated the final results in the forthcoming Final Award. The Tribunal rejected the Chinese argument made in the Position Paper that the Parties' dispute was actually about the delimitation of a maritime boundary between them and therefore excluded from the Tribunal's jurisdiction by virtue of a prior declaration made by China in 2006. On the contrary, the Tribunal held that each of the Submissions by the Philippines reflected disputes between the two States concerning the "interpretation or application" of the Convention. In addition, it also found no other parties were indispensable to the proceedings.

[6] Press Release, October 29, 2015, Arbitration between Republic of the Philippines and the People's Republic of China, p. 1. The final Award, handed down by the Tribunal on July 12, 2016, made the same point, in Sec. III, Para. 130.
[7] Ibid.

Hence, it disallowed the proposed interventions by Vietnam and Republic of China (ROC)/Taiwan.

Parenthetically, the procedural part predetermined the final rulings on merits, if the Tribunal remained truthful, as it did, to the Convention. For instance, the Philippines asked the Tribunal to rule that "China is not entitled to exercise 'historic rights' over the waters, seabed, and subsoil *beyond the limits of its entitlements under the Convention* in the areas encompassed within its so-called 'nine-dash line'" (emphasis added). And, true to the letter and spirit of the Convention, the Tribunal did so rule, exactly. There would be no other way in a truthful interpretation of the Convention, given the fact that it did not provide for rights over "historic waters."

The Tribunal's UNCLOS-Based Final Award Against China: A Critique

In its Final Award, the Arbitral Tribunal narrowly conceived its role in the present case as one concerned only with the "interpretation or application" of the UNCLOS III, as per Art. 287 of the Convention. The Tribunal reiterated that it was "not empowered to address [the] question" of sovereignty.[8] This restriction, which was admittedly true, derived from two sources. One was the UNCLOS III itself, which is not concerned with issues of sovereignty. The other was the *compromis d'arbitrage* under which the Tribunal was constituted. With the nonparticipation of China, the terms in the *compromis d'arbitrage*, concerning the human composition and competence of the Tribunal plus the rules of law and principles the Tribunal was empowered to apply were, therefore, all set unilaterally by the Philippines, following its exclusionary choices geared toward a game plan to win. Thus, the cards were stacked against China in favor of the Philippines from the moment China delivered its refusal to participate. This is a point that, to my knowledge, has not been made by any commentator, of any nationality, on the reasons why the Philippines won the case. But, it is worth serious consideration, and, in fact, a lesson for China to take to heart in introspection.

[8] Para. 262(b) of the final Award reiterated the same point that it had made in its earlier award on Jurisdiction and Admissibility.

The final Award spelled out the Tribunal's rulings on the three interrelated matters reported in the preliminary Award on Jurisdiction and Admissibility, as summarized earlier in this chapter. More specifically, the Final Award stated that the Tribunal could find no legal underpinning in the UNCLOS III for China's historic-rights claim associated with its 9-dash line — because the Convention is totally silent on the historic waters issue. It held that China's claims to historic rights, or other sovereign rights or jurisdiction, with respect to the maritime area enclosed by the 9-dash line, are contrary to the Convention and without lawful effects, to the extent that they exceeded the limits allowed by the Convention. All this reasoning, however, would not be readily understandable unless we come to grips with the inherent *definitional game* that the Tribunal was in fact playing. We need to discern and dissect the minute conceptual differentiations and linguistic manipulations that were manifest in the final Award, in order to fully comprehend why and how the Tribunal drew the conclusions it did. If generalizations can be made at a highest order, five such points, reflecting this definitional game, underscored the Tribunal's answers and conclusions:

1. That historic rights are defined exclusively as rights over resources, living and nonliving
2. That historic rights as such do not carry sovereignty
3. That China's "historical knowledge" (sic) concerning the islands, such as the Spratlys, "has nothing to do with the question of whether China has historically had rights to living and non-living resources beyond the limits of the territorial sea in the South China Sea, hence irrelevant to matters before the Tribunal"
4. Waters and islands are two separate domains. "Waters of the South China Sea cannot lead to rights with respect to the islands there"
5. China's historical exercise was an "exercise of freedoms" on the high seas permitted to all nations by international law[9]

The Tribunal made at least two important rulings that are either unconscionable due to the obvious invidious factual falsehood or,

[9] Sec. V, Final Award, Paras. 256–257; 265–267.

even worse, legally untenable. First, the unconscionable, and factually untrue, ruling was the one in which the Tribunal said it could find "no evidence that China had historically exercised exclusive control over the waters of their resources." Therefore, "the Tribunal concluded that there was no legal basis for China to claim *historic rights* to resources within the sea area falling within the nine-dash line" (emphasis added).[10] On this, it must be pointed out, the Tribunal was confusing "historic rights" and "historic waters," which, as Clive R. Symmons sternly urged, must be distinguished one from the other; they are not coextensive, or coterminous. "Historic rights" concerned with, for instance, high-seas fishing do not give States "acquisition over the sea by prescription," but "historic waters" do.[11] If the Tribunal, composed of professional jurists (including four former judges and one professor of international law), knew the difference, and yet characterized China's "historic rights" as title to fishing and resources, the ulterior motive is obvious, and far from above reproach. In fact, it is subject to severe challenge, and truly condemnable.

Second, the other, and legally untenable, ruling of the Tribunal was found in the Award's statement: "Any historic rights China may have had to the living and non-living resources within the nine-dash line were *superseded* ... by the limits of maritime zones provided by the Convention" (emphasis added).[12] Later, the wording was modified, so that China's ratification of the UNCLOS III in 1996 "did not extinguish historic rights in the waters of the South China Sea. Rather, China *relinquished* the freedoms of the high seas that it had previously utilized with respect to living and non-living resources of certain sea areas which the international community had collectively determined to place within the gambit of the exclusive economic zones of other States" (emphasis added).[13]

But, in the concluding part of Section V in the Final Award, the Tribunal returned to the original notion, that "to the extent China

---

[10] Sec. V, Para. 258, and so on.

[11] Clive R. Symmons, *Historical Waters in the Law of the Sea* (Leidon/Boston, MA: Martinus Nijhoff, 2008), p. 5.

[12] Ibid., Sec V, Para. 262.

[13] Ibid., Para. 271.

had historic rights to resources in the waters of the South China Sea, such rights were *extinguished* to the extent they were incompatible with the exclusive economic zones provided in the Convention" (emphasis added).[14] In other words, China's historic rights established over the centuries (as illustrated in Chapter 2) were, according to the Arbitral Tribunal, "extinguished" by the 1982 Convention.

This allegation, and the thought behind it, goes diametrically opposed to a tradition established since 1930 and reconfirmed by the 1958 Geneva Convention on the Law of the Sea, to the effect that historic rights over a maritime area shall not be extinguished by subsequent treaties.[15]

That said, we can almost sense what the rest of the Award had to say about the questions raised by the Philippine Submissions, since the Tribunal lopsidedly gauged everything exclusively against what the UNCLOS III provided, or did not provide, on all matters in the dispute. Two examples would serve to prove this point. Both are in the third category of the matters raised in the Philippine Submissions for the Tribunal's rulings, namely whether certain Chinese activities in the SCS violated the convention, and so on.

One, on the question raised in the Philippines' Submission No. 9, regarding alleged failure by China to prevent its nationals from exploring the Philippines' living resources, the Tribunal typically ruled:

> China has, through the operation of its marine surveillance vessels in tolerating and failing to exercise due diligence to prevent fishing by Chinese flagged vessels at Mischief Reef and Second Thomas Shoal in May 2013, failed to exhibit due regard for the Philippines' sovereign rights with respect to fisheries in its exclusive economic zone. Accordingly, China has breached its obligations under Article 58(3) of the Convention.[16]

---

[14] Ibid., Sec. V(F)(d)(278), p. 117.

[15] "Juridical Regime of Historic Waters Including Historic Bays," a study prepared by the U.N. International Law Commission, Doc. A/CN.4/143, p. 12; as discussed in Chapter 3.

[16] Final Award Sec. VII (B)(5)d)(757), p. 297.

If anyone is puzzled by why the Tribunal, in its discussion of who had violated who else's rights, failed to do a prior examination of the conflict between the Philippines' claim regarding its exclusive economic zone, on the one hand, and China's historic-waters claim, on the other, the answer should be self-apparent. For, it would be impossible to do such a comparison within the framework of the UNCLOS III.

Two, the other example concerned the future conduct of the Parties, as raised in the Philippine Submission No. 15, on which the Tribunal ruled: "Both Parties are obliged to comply with the Convention, including its provisions regarding the resolution of disputes, and to respect the rights and freedoms of other States *under the Convention*" (emphasis added).[17]

Unmistakably, for China, this would be like a one-way street, because its historic-waters rights would not be equally respected, much less protected, under the Convention — because, to reiterate, the Convention does not provide for historic-waters rights, let alone their protection.

Recourse for China Following the Negative Arbitral Award: Damage Control Needed

The damage to China wrought by the negative final Award of the Arbitral Tribunal, despite the PRC's denunciation and refusal to accept it, cannot be lightly dismissed or ignored. An incomplete tally shows that 10 States were on record as officially supporting the results of the arbitration. Other than Vietnam, all the others are the world's major powers, including the United States, United Kingdom, France, Germany, Italy, Canada, Australia, India, and Japan.

Fourteen others, on the other hand, were opposed to the Arbitral Tribunal's final award. But, discounting ROC/Taiwan whose position duplicates that of the PRC, this group consists mainly of smaller countries like Myanmar, Togo, Syria, Siri Lanka, Niger, Tajikistan,

[17] Ibid., Sec. IX (D)(201), p. 469.

Kenya, Liberia, Vanuatu, and Cambodia, with the exception of Russia, South Africa, and Pakistan.[18]

Scarcely, however, can the far-reaching effects be fully fathomed by this "popularity contest," as it were, between how many countries were or were not in support of the Tribunal's rulings against China. For instance, James Kraska, at the U.S. Naval War College, thinks that Vietnam already "benefits" from the SCS arbitration.[19] The scofflaw stigma consequentially leveled on China has already swayed the opinions, nay, poisoned the minds, of many a mainstream academic in America. One article, for example, by a seasoned China expert, published in the widely respected *Foreign Affairs*, began in the first paragraph with these words: "China . . . has defied international law."[20]

The stigma will not go away simply by Beijing's dismissal or denunciation of the Award, as it has tried. It must be dealt with head-on by adjudicative means. But, since we are going to discuss this point at length in the final chapter, in the context of the search for a possible resolution of the SCS disputes, we should not duplicate the discussion here.

Article 11 of Annex 7 of UNCLOS III, on the "Finality of Award," states that "the award shall be final and without appeal." However, Article 12 provides for a procedure which may serve to offer what amounts to a factual "appeal" opportunity, though without the name. Article 12 is on the modality of resolving a controversy regarding interpretation or implementation — in this case, the controversy over the interpretation of the Tribunal's final Award *qua* application of the UNCLOS III — if a controversy should occur. Art. 12(2) provides: "Any such controversy may be submitted to another court or tribunal under Article 287 by agreement of all the parties to

[18] Tally available in "Philippines vs. China," in Wikipedia, the free encyclopedia.

[19] James Kraska, "Vietnam Benefits from the South China Sea Arbitration," retrieved August 30, 2016 maritimeawarenessproject.org/.../Vietnam-benefits-from-the-souh-china-sea-arbitration.

[20] Susan Shirk, "Trump and China," *Foreign Affairs*, vol. 96, no. 2 (March/April 2017).

the dispute." And, Art. 287 of the Convention offers a choice of four such forums:

1. The ITLOS, established in accordance with Annex VI
2. The ICJ
3. An arbitral tribunal constituted in accordance with Annex VII
4. A special arbitral tribunal constituted in accordance with Annex XII

Besides, the preamble of the UNCLOS III proclaims that "matters not regulated by this Convention continue to be governed by the rules and principles of general international law." Since the Tribunal in the arbitration between the Philippines and China did not follow this stipulation but arrived at its rulings totally in disregard of the "rules and principles of general international law," on the matter of historic waters, China has a right to seek an "interpretation" from one of the abovementioned four forums, of which I prefer the ICJ. In its application for interpretation, China can raise a prior question about the legitimacy of the Arbitral Tribunal's award reached without regard to the admonition of the Convention's preamble, as just noted. Thus, it calls for an "interpretation" of the Tribunal's Award. Then it can restructure the questions to be addressed from the standpoint of general international law, to break away from the trap set by the unilateral discretion of the Philippines, as a result of the nonparticipation of China.

In the eighth, and concluding, chapter, we are going to spell out how China could proceed with this request for interpretation as an ersatz appeal procedure without the name. We should stop here and not steal the thunder from that exercise.

Chapter

5

Before the Storm: U.S.–China Relations in Retrospect — Patterns and Antecedents

Amidst the ballyhoos over the current contest between the rising China and the reigning U.S. superpower, which was rendered more acute under the Presidency of Donald Trump, many Western analysts have begun to sound their alarm that the two powers are "destined for war." In fact, that is the title of a new book by Graham Allison, a seasoned political scientist at Harvard University's Kennedy School. The book's subtitle — Can America and China Escape Thucydides's Trap? — catches a wide concern of all peace-loving people.[1]

The so-called Thucydides Trap is named after the great ancient Greek historian Thucydides (c. 460–c. 400 BC), who wrote about the Peloponnesian War. It was, in his view, the rise of Athens and the fear it instilled in Sparta that ignited the war. As if to confirm this hidden

[1] Graham Allison, *Destined for War: Can America and China Escape Thucydides's Trap?* (Boston: Houghton Mifflin Harcourt, 2017).

logic, it was found, 12 out of 16 similar cases in the past 500 years — in which a rising power edged forward to a contest, often involuntary, with the existing dominant power — ended violently.[2] Hence, some analysts, and governments alike, have ventured to liken the current U.S.–China square-off to the Germany–Britain confrontation before World War I,[3] recalling the contest between Athens and Sparta on the eve of the Peloponnesian War.

The question for us is: Can this be true? Before looking for a sensible answer, however, we need to review America's relations with China in the crucibles of history, to probe a prior question, viz.: Why did the doomsday specter, as such, appear now, and not before, not even during the Cold War era? The habitual, cut-and-dry, answer is that China's rise is only in the last three decades or so, when it has risen much faster and higher than any previous example, to become the world's second largest economy (with the prospect of overtaking the United States in another few years); it is already the largest trading nation in the world since 2014. But, this perfunctory answer suffers from a huge, deplorable, and commonly seen ignorance of relevant history: For over a millennium (713–1820 AD), China wielded the unbroken record of having the world's largest gross domestic product (GDP). According to the data meticulously kept by the British economic historian, Angus Maddison,[4] which confirmed earlier studies,[5]

---

[2] Ibid., 41ff.

[3] In one similar example, Shinzo Abe, Prime Minister of Japan, drew the same analogy, while comparing the relationship between an "assertive" China and a "peaceful" Japan, at the 2014 Davos Economic Forum. "Shinzo Abe's History Lesson Haunts Davos," *Wall Street Journal,* January 28, 2014. He was immediately rebuffed, however, by Alex Lo, "Shinzo Abe's First World War Analogy Is Not So Great," *South China Morning Post* (SCMP, Hong Kong), June 8, 2014.

[4] Angus Maddison, *The World Economy: Historical Statistics* (Paris: OECD, 2003); and *Contours of the World Economy: 1-2030 AD* (Oxford: University of Oxford Press, 2007); also, James C. Hsiung, *China into Its Second Rise* (Singapore: World Scientific, 2012), pp. 47–70.

[5] Eric Jones, *Growth Recurring, Economic Change in World History* (Oxford: Clarendon Press, 1988); Andre Gunder Frank, *Re-Orient: Global Economy in the Asian Age* (Berkley: University of California Press, 1998), pp. 52–130.

China's GDP during the millennium was larger than the combined total of Europe. And, for five centuries (15th through early 19th), China presided over a "tribute system" of international relations of its own, outside the post-Westphalia system.[6]

Armed with this knowledge, you may ask: Why didn't the specter of a sinister "China threat" appear previously in history? A sub-question is: Why was China not considered a contestant for power to America until now? The answers are inherent in a review of the relevant history.

American–Chinese Relations and U.S. China Policy: Patterns in Historical Light

Much of the Chinese millennium (713–1820), referred to above, took place before the settlement of Europeans in the Americas that began only after the discovery of the New World in 1492. However, not until 1889, when it acquired the Spanish colony of the Philippines as a trophy from the Spanish–American War, did America turn its more serious official attention to Asia. Until then, America had relatively little to do with Asia, although, as one historian facetiously noted, the American colonists did "consume a great quantity of Chinese tea."[7] The substance thrown into Boston Harbor on December 16, 1773, in the iconic event known as the Boston Tea Party triggering the outbreak of the American Revolution — some 90,000 pounds (45 tons) of tea — had been shipped from China by the (British) East India Company.[8]

Even before the opening of Japan to U.S. trade by Commodore Matthew Perry in 1853, private American firms were drawn to the

---

[6] David Kang, *East Asia Before the West: Five Centuries of Trade and Tribute* (New York: Columbia University Press, 2010).

[7] Te-Kong Tong, "The Manchus and the Yankees, 1784–1911" (paper presented at the Asian-American Assembly for Policy Research meeting, City College of New York, CUNY, New York, April 29, 1977), p. 2.

[8] Benjamin L. Carp, *Defiance of the Patriots: The Boston Tea Party and Making of America*, chap. 1 (New Haven: Yale University Press, 2010).

prospect of the "illimitable" market in China. Missionary zeal was also aroused to the huge potential flock the christian church would hope to tend to, among the four hundred million Chinese.[9]

The Unfolding of U.S. China Policy in Historical Contexts: Treaties and Congressional Acts

Diplomatic relations between the American Republic and the Manchu empire of China, begun since the early 19th century, paved the way for the future development of their relationship for over a century, punctuated by the twists and turns of China's domestic politics. They unfolded against a backdrop of three currents sweeping across China and Asia in general.

1. The first was the steady decline of the Manchu empire in China, caught as it was in a downward dynastic cycle, and squeezed by the combination of a population explosion,[10] an unending series of revolts (the most debilitating one was the Taiping Rebellion, 1851–1864, which almost toppled the Manchu government), and the impact of the relentless multiple encroachments by European powers (and Japan) that resulted in what was often described as China's century-long national humiliation that

[9] Peter Parker, a long serving and influential member of the American legation in China, advocated a policy geared toward the missionary interest, and for that reason supported the British gunboat diplomacy, so that a "kingdom of God" could be built upon the ruins of the Chinese empire after its potential destruction. Edward Vose Gulick, *Peter Parker and the Opening of China* (Cambridge: Harvard University Press, 1973), pp. 166–195. For American missionary interest in China at the time, see Te-Kong Tong, *United States Diplomacy in China, 1844–1860* (Seattle: University of Washington Press, 1964), 23f.

[10] In 1651, at the beginning of the Manchu Dynasty, China had a population of no more than 60 million, but by 1849, it had increased almost seven times to 413 million. Lucian Pye, *China: An Introduction*, 2nd ed. (Boston: Little Brown, 1978), p. 103.

eventually swept the Communist Revolution to victory by the middle of the 20th century.[11]

2. The second current was the spread of European expansion and colonialism in Asia ("imperialism," as the Communists would call it).[12]
3. The third was the slow extension of the American frontierism across the Pacific, including a religious and political proselytizing spirit.[13]

The evolution of America's official relations with China can be seen from the treaties they concluded, beginning with the first bilateral Treaty of Wanghia, in 1844. This instrument confirmed what China had already extended to the United States, following the example of the Chinese concessions to the British in the Treaty of Nanking (Nanjing) of 1842,[14] which ended the Opium War — a war that was brought on by China's resistance to the British attempt to ram their India-grown opium down the collective Chinese throat.[15] The Wanghia Treaty formalized the privileges enjoyed by the Americans, such as the opening of the five trading ports, extraterritorial rights (by which Americans who committed crimes in China shall be "tried and punished by the American consul or other public functionary,"

---

[11] Lucian W. Pye, *China: An Introduction*, 4th ed. (New York: HarperCollins, 1991), pp. 83–173; Franklin W. Houn classified these encroachments into 15 categories, including China's loss of the right to determine and set its tariffs, as the head of the Chinese Customs Office had to be a Briton appointed from London, *A Short History of Chinese Communism* (Englewood Cliffs: Prentice Hall, 1973), pp. 6–7.

[12] *David Scott, China and the International System, 1840–1949: Power, Presence, and Perceptions in a Century of Humiliation* (Albany: *SUNY Press, 2008), 111ff.*

[13] William Appleman Williams, "The Frontier Thesis and American Foreign Policy," *Pacific Historical Review* 24 (1955): 379–395.

[14] The Treaty of Nanking was the first international instrument by which a foreign power imposed unilateral terms on China, hence setting an example for all future unequal treaties China had to sign in the 19th century. William L. Tung, *China and the Powers* (Dobbs Ferry: Oceana, 1970), 20ff.

[15] In the British Parliament, however, the war was described as one to open China to foreign trade.

beyond the reach of Chinese law), fixed tariffs, and most-favored-nation (MFN) treatment.[16] As a goodwill gesture, the Chinese Government agreed that the treaty might be subject to revision in 12 years.[17] One distinct feature in the Treaty was the right of Americans to build churches and hospitals in China.

The Treaty, in retrospect, marked America's role on the China scene, as a Johnny-come-lately, ever eager to expand its opportunities, often in competition with the European old hands (and the Japanese). Later, by the MFN clause, the United States, like Russia, was able to benefit from the same concessions that the much weakened Manchu Court was required to grant in the 1858 Treaty of Tientsin (Tianjing), capitulating to the demands of Britain and France after their joint expedition defeated the Chinese. The four separate but parallel Treaties of Tientsin, signed by each of the four powers with China provided identical terms, although neither America nor Russia participated in the Anglo-Franco expedition. As a result, America enjoyed the same new privileges like the opening of additional ports and of the Yangtze River to foreign shipping up to Hankow, inland trade and travel, and residence of foreign envoys in the Chinese capital, not to mention the legalization of opium imports into China.[18]

Another agreement, known as the Burlingame Treaty, signed between the United States and China in 1868, contained an anti-immigration clause, reflecting the rising anti-Chinese labor sentiments in America, especially in the Pacific region, at the time. While Chinese labor was in great demand on farms and in industries,[19] the Democratic-associated labor organizations were alarmed by the Chinese competition in the labor market; and mounted a bitter

---

[16] Tung, *China and the Powers*, 22.

[17] For the text of the Wanghia Treaty, see *Treaties, Conventions, etc., between China and Foreign States* (Shanghai: Statistical Department of the Inspectorate-General of Customs, 1908), I, 486.

[18] For full text of the Tientsin Treaties, see Edward Herslett, *Treaties, etc., Between China and Foreign Powers* (1908), I, 540–552.

[19] In particular, Chinese labor was especially needed in the construction of the Central Pacific Railroad.

opposition campaign against it.[20] Shortly after the signing of the 1868 Treaty, the American anti-Chinese movement reached a new high. In the Election year of 1880, both the Democrats and the Republicans registered in their platforms various pledges against Chinese immigration. In 1882, over the veto of President Chester Arthur, Congress adopted a bill that would bar the immigration of Chinese laborers for 10 years and prohibit granting citizenship to the Chinese.[21] This heralded a series of anti-Chinese laws adopted by Congress known collectively as Chinese Exclusion Acts.[22] As an irony of history, these discriminatory laws proved to be the antecedents of the executive decrees signed by the newly inaugurated President Trump in early 2017 to ban immigrants into America. The only differences are that the 2017 bans were fiats issued by the country's chief executive, rather than acts of Congress, and that they were immediately challenged in courts, thus effectively mollified by judicial means.

Genesis of the Open Door Policy[23]

Until the time of the Tientsin Treaties of 1858, the United States' China policy followed the tenet of a layback "peaceful cooperation" with regard to the other foreign powers.[24] And, it could do so because its interests were protected by the NFN guarantee in the Wanghia Treaty, provided that a minimal peace prevailed within China. However, the Anglo-Franco War of 1884–1885 that brought about the Tientsin Treaties, and, more in particular, the Japanese war against China 10 years hence, shook the "peace" premise to its foundation. America's next best bet was to opt for a defensive neutrality.

[20] Mary Roberts Coolidge, *Chinese Immigration* (New York: Holt, 1909; reprinted by the Ch'eng-wen Publishing, 1968), 378ff.

[21] Ibid., 96ff.

[22] Ibid., 302ff; 168ff.

[23] The policy was so-called in order to keep China "open" to America the late comer, in competition with the European powers.

[24] William L. Marcy MSS, Manuscript Section, Library of Congress, LXXV, 49475, cited in Tong, U.S. Diplomacy in China, see note 7, pp. 199–201.

After all, it was not yet a Far East power, and its commercial interests did not warrant any deeper involvement.[25]

By the end of the 19th century, however, with the conclusion of the Spanish–American War and its acquisition of the Philippines, the United States became a Far Eastern power almost overnight.[26] Its commercial interests in China almost doubled in a matter of a few years.[27]

On the other hand, the fortunes of the Manchu Dynasty in China had sunk to its nadir. The defeat in the 1895 war with Japan, an Asian power that used to be at the receiving end of Chinese culture, demoralized the Manchu Court. But, it strengthened the hand of the Empress Dowager Tzu-hsi (Cixi) in her meddling in Court politics, thus dooming the "Hundred Day Reforms" initiated by the young Emperor Guanghsu (Guangxu), whom himself was placed under house arrest by the Empress Dowager.[28] Taking advantage of the chaos, the powers took control and established their respective spheres of influence in different parts of China: Russia in the northeast,[29] Britain in Central China,[30] and France in the south.[31] Italy, Portugal, and Belgium also attempted to take their respective shares from the dying Celestial Empire, such as rights in railroad

---

[25] Jeffrey M. Dorwart, *The Pigtail War: America in the Sino-Japanese War of 1894–1895* (Amherst: University of Massachusetts Press, 1975), pp. 29–42.

[26] Julius W. Pratt, *Expansionists of 1898, the Acquisition of Hawaii and the Spanish Islands* (Chicago: Quadrangle Books, 1964), 230ff; *A History of U.S. Foreign Policy* (Englewood Cliffs: Prentice-Hall, 1972), 279ff.

[27] Charles Beard, *The Idea of National Interest, an Analytical Study of American Foreign Policy* (Chicago: Quadrangle Books, 1966), 89ff.

[28] Li Chien-nung, *The Political History of China*, trans. and ed. by Ssu-yu Teng and Jeremy Ingalls (Princeton: Princeton University Press, 1971), pp. 155–163.

[29] Oliver Edmund Clubb, *China and Russia, the "Great Game"* (New York: Columbia University Press, 1971), 125ff; also, Peter S. H. Tang, *Russian and Soviet Policy in Manchuria and Outer Mongolia, 1911–1931* (London: Duke University Press, 1959), 30ff.

[30] Hosa Ballou Morse, *The International Relations of the Chinese Empire: The Period of Conflict, 1834–1860* (London: Longmans, Green, 1910), III, 120f; William Leonard Langer, *The Diplomacy of Imperialism, 1890–1902,* chap. XXI (New York: Knopf, 1935), II; The Boxer Rebellion, 677ff.

[31] Morse, *International Relations*, pp. 102–127.

construction, mining, and the organization of influential consortiums, and so on. In addition, China's frontier regions like Tibet, Yunnan, Sinkiang (Xinjiang), and Mongolia were all coveted by the powers and are vulnerable to their penetration, even occupation, in the foreseeable future.[32]

As a belated participant in the international power game, the United States was watching all this with dismay. The U.S. envoy in Beijing, Edwin H. Conger, was wondering if the United States should also "own and control a good coaling station on the Chinese coast" or to be a "party to the division and a sharer in the assets." Even so, he realized, "it may be too late" for America.[33] With its commercial interests next only to Britain's in total value, the United States could not afford to be excluded from any part of China, an outcome that would result from a partition of the country by the powers. Thus, a status quo in China ("open" to the American Johnny-come-lately) would, therefore, best serve the purpose of the United States.[34]

With the full understanding of his British counterpart, U.S. Secretary of State John Hay sent off a series of official notes, known as the Open Door Notes, to the treaty powers, from September 6 through November 17, 1899, asking them to reach a common understanding on China. The powers, Hay suggested, should enjoy perfect equality of treatment for their commerce and navigation in their respective "sphere of influence/interests" within the Chinese empire, and let China preserve its administrative system in the various foreign spheres of influence. The reactions to Hay's notes from the treaty powers varied, ranging from the British who declared a reservation about Hong Kong and Kowloon to the others such as Germany, France, Japan, and Italy, each of which would accept the U.S.

---

[32] Ibid., Chap. V: The Impending Break-up of China.

[33] Conger to Hay, March 1, 1899, in Diplomatic Dispatches, Microfilmed by the U.S. National Archives service (DD-USNA), 106: 155.

[34] Cf. Samuel Flagg Bemis, *A Diplomatic History of the United States* (New York: Heny Holt, 1945), 483ff; also, A. Whitney Griswold, *The Far Eastern Policy of the United States*, chap. II (Yale University Press, 3rd printing, 1962), pp. 36–86; Writing the Open Door Notes.

suggestion if the others would do the same. The only demurer was Russia, but not for long; it relented shortly thereafter.[35]

However, Russia could not be stopped from its meddling in Manchuria (English name for northeast China) and expanding its sphere of influence there. Nor Japan's extension of its penetration into the southern part of the region, operating from nearby Korea, which had been reduced to a Japanese colony after it was ceded by China at the end of the war of 1895. The worst outcome, certifying the failure of the United States' Open Door initiative of Secretary John Hay, was the Russo-Japanese War of 1905. The fact that the war, between two foreign powers, was fought on Chinese territory (Manchuria), blatantly flouted the "territorial integrity" principle that the Open Door Notes sought to urge on the powers on behalf of China. At the Portsmouth peace talks, which President Theodore Roosevelt brokered, none of the three powers (the United States, Russia, and Japan) paid any serious attention to China, many of whose citizens lost their lives and/or properties when the Russo-Japanese war was fought on their homeland.

At Portsmouth, Teddy Roosevelt did everything possible to save the Russians in Manchuria. As a result of the conference, the region was to be divided between Russian influence in the north and Japanese influence in the south of Manchuria.[36] This arrangement was itself a retreat from the United States' Open Door Policy. Nonetheless, the United States undertook a further retreat by signing a series of supplementary treaties with the rising imperialist power of Japan, at the expense of China and Korea. In the summer of 1905, the President gave his approval to the secret Taft–Katsura Agreement, under which the United States recognized Japan's suzerainty over Korea, in exchange for Japan's assurance of nonaggression toward the Philippines.[37]

---

[35] U.S. State Department, Foreign Relations of the United States (FRUS), 1899, 128–143.

[36] Morse, *International Relations*, see note 29, III, 426ff.

[37] Charles A. Beard, *The Open Door at Home* (New York: Macmillan, 1935), 179ff; David H. Burton, *Theodore Roosevelt* (New York: Twayne Publishers, 1972), p. 128.

Three years later, in 1908, the President beat another retreat when the secret Root–Takahira Agreement was concluded. Under this new pact, while Japanese nonaggression pledge against the Philippines was reconfirmed, the United States skillfully evaded its responsibility for upholding the Open Door doctrine in Manchuria. While the Open Door's key tenet was to seek the respect for China's territorial integrity, the word "territorial" was deleted from the text of the Root–Takahira Agreement.[38]

The Nine-Power Treaty: Codification of the Open Door Doctrine

After the failure at the Paris Peace Conference (1919) to settle China's Shantung (Shandong) question[39] and other problems of the Pacific, the United States began making plans in 1920 for another international meeting, which materialized in the Washington Conference of 1920–1922. It had a dual agenda, one related to naval disarmament, and the other to problems of the Far East. For the latter agenda, the conference was attended by nine powers with interests in the Far East and the Pacific, namely: Britain, the United States, France, Italy, Japan, China, Belgium, the Netherlands, and Portugal. The Chinese delegation presented a nine-point proposal, asking the participants to honor China's territorial integrity and political independence; to desist from concluding treaties among themselves that would affect China; to respect its neutrality in future wars; to remove all limitations on its political, jurisdictional, and administrative freedom; to review all foreign special rights, immunities, and concessions in China; and to set time limits to its commitments.[40]

---

[38] Michael H. Hunt, *Frontier Defense and the Open Door: Manchuria in Chinese American Relations, 1895–1911* (New Haven: Yale University Press, 1973), p. 130.

[39] China had entered World War I with the specific hope that upon Germany's defeat its hold on Shantung (Shandong) would be relinquished and the peninsula would be returned to China. But, at the Versailles Conference, Japan demanded to take over Shantung from the defeated Germany.

[40] Immanuel Hsu, *The Rise of Modern China*, 6th ed. (New York: Oxford University Press, 2000), p. 532; Tung *China and the Powers* and see note 13, pp. 185–188.

Under U.S. sponsorship, the nine points in the Chinese proposal were consolidated into four general principles, which found ultimate expression in the Nine-Power Treaty (February 6, 1922). The signatories agreed to respect China's territorial integrity and political independence; to renounce further attempts to seek spheres of influence; to respect its neutrality in time of war; and to honor equal commercial opportunity for all. Separately, the powers agreed to close on January 1, 1923, all foreign postal offices in China except in the leased territories, and to let China increase the import tariffs from the actual 3.5% to 5% ad valorem.[41] This was the first time that the Open Door doctrine was reaffirmed in treaty form. Besides, and more importantly, the traditional practice by the powers to establish spheres of influence in China was terminated. As one commentator points out, the only defect of the treaty was its lack of a provision for sanctions against its breach by any signatory. Hence, when Japan commenced full-scale aggression in China, in July 1937, the Nine-Power Conference held in Brussels in November failed dismally to do anything to uphold the terms of the Nine-Power Treaty.[42]

From Japan's Aggression in China to Its Attack on Pearl Harbor

The Japanese militarists' plan to conquer China by piecemeal, under the Amau (Amo) doctrine,[43] started with the Kwantung Army's intrepid expansionism in Manchuria. It took an event, known as the Mukden Incident (or, the "September 18th Incident" in Chinese), to bring it to light for the outside world.[44] The event was engineered by

---

[41] Ibid.

[42] Tung, *China and the Powers* and see note 13, p. 188.

[43] For the "Amau Statement," 17 April 1934. U.S. State Department, *Foreign Relations of the United States*: *Japan, 1931–1941* (Washington: Government Printing Office, 1943), I, pp. 224–225.

[44] Robert H. Ferrell, "The Mukden Incident: September 18–19, 1931," *Journal of Modern History* 27, no. 1 (1955): 66–72.

the Japanese Kwantung Army, whose ranks were deployed in the region under the pretext of protecting the South Manchurian Railroad that the Japanese had helped build in the region. Using the alibi that the Mukden train station was blown up by Chinese saboteurs at 9 o'clock, on the night of September 18, 1931, the Kwantung Army swooped down to take control of, first, the city of Shenyang (Mukden, in English), and later the entire Manchuria — a fertile land about two and a half times bigger than California, or as big as Texas, Alabama, and Louisiana added together.

After China appealed to the League of Nations, the Lytton Commission sent by the League came in for inspection, only to find that the 9:30 p.m. train arrived on time, thus exposing the Japanese hoax (lie?) about the train station blow-up.[45]

China also turned to the United States for help. In a note sent on January 7, 1932, the U.S. Secretary of State Henry L. Stimson notified both China and Japan that he was confident that the League would ultimately find a solution, and announced that the United States would not recognize the fruits of aggression. This came to be known as the Stimson Doctrine of Non-Recognition,[46] which amounted to a de facto retreat from the Open Door commitment enshrined in the Nine-Power Treaty of 1922, calling for respect for China's territorial integrity and political independence.

After its occupation of the entire Manchuria, the Japanese established a puppet Manchukuo (Kingdom of Manchu) regime, to run the administration of the region, displacing the Chinese. The Kwantung Army then extended its feelers southward, to spread Japanese control into North China. When it met strong resistance from the Chinese side, an incident at Lugouqiao (known in English as the Marco Polo Bridge), some 20 km (or 13 miles) southwest of Beijing, on July 7, 1937, ignited an explosion that erupted into a

---

[45] LIANG Jing-dun, *Jiuyiba shibian shishu* (A Historical Account of the September 18 [Mukden] Incident) (Jamaica: Center for Asian Studies, St. Johns University, 1964), 315ff.

[46] Richard N. Current, "The Stimson Doctrine and the Hoover Doctrine," *American Historical Review* 59, no. 3 (April 1954): 513–542.

full-fledged war, known in China as the War of Resistance (to Japanese aggression), lasting for eight more years (until September 9, 1945).[47]

For the first four years, the unprepared and under-gunned China was fighting the Japanese alone, without international aid or sympathy, while the West was preoccupied with the Nazi threat in Europe. Likewise, U.S. attention was diverted to Europe, even more so after Germany invaded Poland in 1939. When the British and French responded by declaring war on Germany, the European phase of World War II (WWII) thus began. John W. Garver described the initial difficulty in the Chinese efforts to win support and sympathy in America. "So overwhelming," he noted, "was the brutality depicted in the movie footage and photos of the bloody massacres of Chinese civilians in Nanking [Nanjing] — most of it taken by participating Japanese soldiers as mementos of the carnage — that the newsreel actually had to be edited and toned down to make it credible to American audiences."[48]

Japan's escalation of the war, facing the Chiang Kai-shek government's refusal to capitulate, led to increasing restrictions of Westerners' activities in China, giving rise to louder Anglo-American protests and a public opinion that was increasingly hostile to Japan. Both the United States and Britain came to realize that China was tying down massive Japanese troops (including draftees from Japanese-controlled Korea), which could be used to expand the war to broader grounds. Interventions by both Britain and the United States would be necessary to defeat Japanese Foreign Minister Hirota's goal of decoupling China from the West, and the efforts of militarists like Ishihara to promote a Pan-Asianism linking China with Japan against the West. Therefore, they came to the conviction that China's heroic fight and sacrifices were, ultimately, helping the West in preventing Japan from

---

[47] Cf. Rana Mitter, *The Forgotten Ally: China's World War II, 1937–1945* (Cambridge: Houghton Mifflin Harcourt, 2015); and James C. Hsiung and Seven I. Levine, eds., *China's Bitter Victory: The War with Japan, 1937–1945* (Armonk: M.E. Sharpe, 1992).

[48] John W. Garver, "China's Wartime Diplomacy," in Hsiung and Levine, eds., *China's Bitter Victory: The War with Japan, 1937–1945* (Armonk: M.E. Sharpe, 1992), p. 12.

establishing a hegemony modeled after Napoleonic France or Hitlerite Germany.[49]

By mid-1938, U.S. policy began to change. Some U.S. officials, like Treasury Secretary Henry Morgenthau, came around to the view that a Japanese domination of China would be detrimental to American interests and, therefore, the Unites States should help keep China from falling under. In December, 1938, Morgenthau approved a $25 million loan to China, which was followed by a second loan of $45 million in early 1940. By then, the United States was feeling the threat more directly from the Axis powers linkage between Japan and Germany, which made the Japanese threat more real. This fear convinced Washington that it should support China in its war efforts against Japan. Once the United States and Great Britain were immersed in a world war, China's strategic importance increased. Now the Anglo-American powers needed China as much as China needed them. Chinese and American leaders struck a bargain, whereby China would continue to fight against Japan in exchange for an appropriate quid pro quo, namely: U.S. aid to China. However, as John Garver points out, "what was essentially an instrumental deal was complicated by suspicions and mistrust on both sides. The Chinese feared that they might again be betrayed by their allies, as had happened so many times before."[50] The Chinese apprehension was due to America's relative casual attitude, as much of Pacific Asia was under the colonial rule of the British, the French, and the Dutch, until the Pearl Harbor attack hit home that U.S. security was actually more directly tied to Asia.

To sustain its broad war efforts logistically, Japan's immediate target by 1941 was the oil fields of the Dutch East Indies (today's Indonesia), whose capture might free Japan from America's economic coercion and, moreover, would provide badly needed oil supplies for Japanese troops on the ground and air force bombers. But access to these oil fields was blocked by the American presence in the

---

[49] Li Yun-han, "The Origins of the War: Background of the Lugouchiao Incident, July 7, 1937," in *Nationalist China During the Sino-Japanese War, 1937–1945*, ed. Paul Sih (Hicksville: Exposition Press, 1977), p. 10.
[50] John Garver, in *China's Bitter Victory* and see note 47, p. 20.

Philippines.[51] The Japanese attack on Pearl Harbor was an action calculated to keep the U.S. Pacific Fleet from interfering with military actions they planned against overseas territories of the Netherlands, Great Britain, and the United States. As for the United States, over the next seven hours, there were coordinated Japanese attacks on the U.S.-held Philippines, and Guam, as well as on Pearl Harbor. The surprise attack came as a profound shock to the American people and led directly to the American entry into WWII in both the Pacific and European theaters.[52] For the Americans, "Pearl Harbor" was a catch-all term for all Japanese attacks on U.S.-held overseas territories.

Probably for the first time in history, Japan's attack on Pearl Harbor forced the United States to consider East Asia in geostrategic terms. More specifically, the erstwhile relationship between the United States the patron and China the client, all of a sudden, morphed into one of copartnership, or allies, fighting on the same side against a common enemy.

FDR's Post–WWII Scenario

By 1944, almost three years after the United States entered the Pacific war, and when victory over Japan was not far from sight, President Franklin D. Roosevelt was starting to plan a strategic scenario for a post–WWII world order of enduring peace. He embraced a strategy outlined in a geopolitical treatise by Professor Nicholas John Spykman of Yale University, published posthumously in 1944, one year after his death. Spykman (October 13, 1893–June 26, 1943) was an American political scientist who was one of the founders of the classical realist school in American foreign policy, transmitting East European political thought into the United States. His *Geography of Peace*, a work on geopolitics and geostrategy, led him to be known as the "godfather of containment."

---

[51] Michael A. Barnhart, *Japan Prepares for Total War: The Search for Economic Security, 1919–1941* (Ithaca: Cornell University Press, 1987), 263ff; David Bergamini, *Japan's Imperial Conspiracy* (New York: William Morrow, 1971), 798ff.

[52] *Jonah Engel Bromwich*, "How Pearl Harbor Shaped the Modern World," *The New York Times, December 7, 2016;* retrieved *March* 25, *2017.*

The thesis advanced by Spykman, known as the Rimland Strategy, postulated that the source of the post–WWII threat to peace would come from the "Heartland Power," a geostrategic term for the Soviet Union, because it occupied the land link between the European and Asian continents. The solution called for America's strategic alignment with the two Rimlands surrounding the Heartland Power on both sides, to contain it — the East Rimland being the Asian subcontinent occupied by China, and the Western Rimland being made up by Western European nations. The Rimlands must be protected at all costs and shored up by the United States, for the sake of peace and stability in the postwar world.[53]

Flowing from the teachings of the Rimland Strategy, therefore, FDR's scenario for Asia was that China (i.e., the Republic of China [ROC] then under the pre-Communist government under Chiang Kai-shek) must be made into a stabilizer in Asia, watching over a potentially resurgent Japan, and an Asian fence against the Heartland Power. At FDR's insistence, and over the objection of Sir Winston Churchill, China was made one of the five permanent members of the U.N. Security Council.[54] Thus, China no longer was a passive "object" (like under the Nine-Power Treaty) or a wartime ally and "partner" (after Pearl Harbor, when the United States entered the war against the common enemy), but a co-player in the defense and maintenance of regional and global peace.

Reversal of the FDR Scenario in Asia After the 1949 Communist Rise in China

The Communist takeover in mainland China in 1949, however, unsettled the plan in the FDR scenario for the postwar era, with far-reaching consequences. China in Communist hands ruined U.S.

---

[53] Nicholas John Spykman, *Geography of the Peace* (New York: Harcourt, Brace, 1944), 60ff.

[54] James C. Hsiung, in Hsiung and Winber Chai, eds., *Asia and U.S. Foreign Policy* (New York: Praeger, 1981), p. 118. For the protection of, and America's alignment with, the Western Europe, the NATO would be an embodiment of the importance of the Western Rimland.

expectations of a staunch ally that would work in concert with Washington to curb Soviet expansionism in the Far East. The People's Republic of China (PRC) was perceived as an extension of Stalin's Communist empire into Asia. More than that, Beijing's militancy, displayed during and beyond the Korean War (1950–1953) also confirmed Washington's worst fears, impelling a reversal of the postwar U.S. policy in East Asia as a whole. In the changed scenario, under Secretary of State John Foster Dulles, peace and stability would depend upon relentless, direct U.S. involvement, with the support of a revived Japan and a fortified (non-Communist) Taiwan kept in the "Free World" camp.

As (mainland) China disappeared from the United States' strategic map, in a reversal of the FDR scenario, surrogates must be found to fill the vacuum left by China as the Asian Rimland, resulting in a network of mutual-security treaties concluded with Japan, South Korea, Taiwan, and the Philippines, among the 42 nations with each of which the United States had entered into a security relationship, not to mention the multilateral Southeast Asia Treaty Organization (SEATO), and the Central Treaty Organization (CENTO) for West Asia. Together, these security pacts were often sarcastically referred to as the products of the "Dullesian Pactomania," named after U.S. Secretary of State John Foster Dulles.[55]

This massive drive confirmed what Hans Morgenthau calls the "turning inside out" from isolationism to globalism in the post–WWII transformation of U.S. foreign policy.[56] The integration of ROC/Taiwan (sometimes nicknamed "island China") into America's interlocking webs of mutual security pacts, built in the 1950s, was premised upon the continuing hostility between the United States and a Soviet-backed Beijing regime, which Washington refused to recognize diplomatically. Containing the PRC was, therefore, part of

[55] Richard H. Immerman, *John Foster Dulles: Piety, Pragmatism, and Power in U.S. Foreign Policy* (Biographies in American Foreign Policy, 1999).

[56] Hans J. Morgenthau, *A New Foreign Policy for the United States* (New York: Praeger, 1969), esp., pp. 15–17; 158–159.

the U.S. efforts toward containing the Soviet empire.[57] Thus, China has undergone another identity change from the former "object" (under the Open Door Policy and the Nine-Power Treaty) to a wartime copartner (after Pearl Harbor) fighting a common enemy, now (after 1949) to an adversary and target of containment in its own right.

Twists and Turns in Post–WWII History and the Reversal of the Reversal of FDR's Scenario

Three ironies marked the twists and turns in post–WWII history, precipitating corresponding changes in U.S. policy toward Asia. The first is that the former enemy Japan, contrary to FDR's blueprint, had to be helped out of defeat to become a U.S. bulwark in East Asia. The second is the unexpectedly short-lived duration of the Beijing–Moscow axis, the collapse of which, from 1957 on, called into question the very rationale of the containment policy toward China (the PRC). The third irony is that when the U.S. policy toward the PRC had to be reversed again in the 1970s, ROC/Taiwan, the U.S. ally of nearly three decades, became a stumbling block for a speedy "normalization" of relations with Beijing. Anxiousness to overcome the stumbling-block dilemma eventually led President Jimmy Carter to abandon (i.e., de-recognize) ROC/Taiwan as from January 1, 1979, when diplomatic relations with the PRC began. Thus, China has returned to the United States' strategic map, in a move that constituted a reversal of the reversal of the FDR scenario.[58]

The Rationale for the Turnaround in the United States' China Policy

A number of factors or considerations may explain the complete turnaround in U.S. attitude and policy toward Beijing, beginning in

[57] Hsiung and Chai, *Asia and U.S. Foreign Policy* and see note 54.
[58] Ibid.

the late 1960s. In addition to the Sino-Soviet split, the Vietnam War fiasco also played a role in impelling a reversal in U.S. policy toward the Asia Pacific, which called for the disengagement of U.S. ground troops from the Asian continent, following Nixon's Guam Doctrine of 1969. The political vacuum to be left by the U.S. pullout had to be filled, to prevent a Soviet penetration into the region. China, by then a nascent nuclear power (since 1964) and hostile to Moscow, came in handy and ready as a counterweight to a Soviet-backed Hanoi, or as a regional stabilizer, if it could be inducted to collaborate with the United States. The idea of China as a regional stabilizer, in a way, harked back to the original FDR design, although the assumed common target had shifted from the post–WWII Japan to the Soviet Union and its Vietnam client, over two decades later.

The new expectations of what China could do in an induced collaboration with the United States were shared by the principal architects of U.S. foreign policy under two Presidents, Nixon and Carter. If the idea of a "China card" was seminal and latent in Kissinger, it became more explicit and operational in Brzezinski, who headed the National Security Council (NSC) under Carter. The course of normalizing U.S. relations with the PRC, I should add, had its additional and, perhaps more compelling, logic in the world's transition from the previous era of dyadic nuclear deterrence to a new era of multiple nuclear deterrence. Let me explain.

As a result of China's entry into the Nuclear Club, certain "rules of the game" in the nuclear deterrence game were drastically transformed. Although not yet a full-fledged nuclear competitor of comparable weight to either the United States or the Soviet Union, China entered the game as a "spoiler," posing a number of grave questions for strategic thinking. First, with three players in the game, it is no longer possible to identify, with the same degree of certitude as before, the origin of a preemptive nuclear first strike, if and when it occurs. A corollary to this "nuclear anonymity" problem is the danger of a catalytic war, one that might be triggered by an initial attack launched by a third nuclear power but simulated as coming from another source. Even when both of these problems are resolved, given sufficient time and the aid of satellite surveillance, another problem that can be called the "victor's inheritance" is insurmountable. That is to say, even if in a bilateral exchange, one of the nuclear powers emerged as the victor over the other, it would still have lost vis-à-vis the standby third party whose nuclear arsenal remains intact.[59] This no-win situation greatly impaired, even nullified, the value of the heretofore prevailing concept of massive "punishment" (or MAD, mutual assured destruction), which had been the central pillar of the erstwhile dyadic (United States–Soviet) deterrence doctrine. It compelled the adoption of an alternative approach premised on the concept of "reward." The age of the new multiple deterrence, in the Kissingerian calculations, would depend on a structure of peace in which all the nuclear adversaries would be "rewarded" for mutual good behavior (for not rocking the nuclear boat).

A few prerequisites, however, must be present for this reward structure to work: (a) Decision makers must take a holistic view of foreign policy, so that losses in one area can be made up by gains in another. Trade-offs as such are extremely important if the reward structure is to work; and they are possible only if the principal national actors are playing a non-zero-sum game. (b) The sources of capability of the principal actors must be differentiated from one another, so that each will have something to offer in the rewarding structure. (c) All principal actors must be involved in an ever-expanding web of interdependence, so that any attempt by one player to hurt another will, by the workings of the close mutual interdependence, boomerang on oneself. (d) There should be no ganging up by any two against the third nuclear player, lest the reward chain be broken.[60]

Although there are other "rules," these are the most essential ones. Again, the reward structure would not work unless all the principals are willing to accept one another as coequals. Hence, the new "rules of the game" contained a logic calling on the United States to

---

[59] Richard Rosecrance, *The Future of the International Strategic System* (San Francisco: Chandler, 1972), pp. 135–140; Hsiung, in Hsiung and Chai, n. 54 above, 119ff.
[60] Ibid., pp. 151–159; Ibid., p. 120.

abandon its previous diplomatic nonrecognition of the PRC, but to accept it officially as a principal actor on the world stage.

Before going on any further, let us pause here to note that the entire Kissingerian détente scenario required (a) a sufficient degree of interdependence, in order for the concept of mutual reward to work, and (b) a compatible willingness on the part of all the principals to accept the same premises. Parenthetically, the element of mutual interdependence may anticipate the difficulty that President Trump had to live with in facing his inability to deliver what he had promised on his campaign trail that he would punish China for America's enormous trade deficit and, moreover, for its alleged currency manipulation practices.

The Kissingerian Premises, Opening of China and Beyond

The opening of China and the modality set for it in the Shanghai Communique signed by President Nixon with Premier Chou En-lai (Zhou Enlai), on February 28, 1972, followed certain premises that were indispensable prerequisites for the rapport thenceforth generated. In retrospect, short of these prerequisites, the United States–China détente would be hardly maintainable. From the hindsight of the post-Cold War developments, this may confirm, and explain, why there have been bumps and dips in U.S. relations with China ever since 1990, which have become even shakier under Donald Trump's presidency.

1. The first premise was that the Sino-Soviet split was irreversible and the United States could take advantage of it by alternately "tilting" to one and then to the other of the two Communist giants. The intent to manipulate one Communist power against the other, nevertheless, undercut the very conceptual foundation of détente that required mutual reward for good behavior (not rocking the nuclear boat). The opening to China in 1972 was a Kissingerian tactic to coerce the Soviets into détente with the United States, taking advantage of the competitive nature of the Sino-Soviet relationship.

2. The second Kissingerian premise had to do with his balance of power preoccupation with China's position in the larger United States–Soviet relationship. Kissinger's blueprint was taken from the 19th-century European diplomatic experience, more especially from the Bismarckian "supergame" design aimed at building a web of balancing bilateral relationships of the major powers, to the exclusion of the lesser actors. A related assumption in the Kissingerian design was about China's relative strength, that is, that it was powerful enough as a counterweight to the Soviets, but not powerful enough to threaten the United States. (As we will see later, this assumption cannot outlive the change of time.)
3. The third Kissingerian premise was that if China was to be encouraged to direct its undivided attention northward, to deal with the Soviets, all its "southern" problems (such as the Vietnam conflict and the Taiwan question) must be resolved for China once and for all.[61]

Post-Watergate and Normalization with China, Until the Soviet Demise

The ground work prepared by the Nixon-Kissinger team was only temporarily overshadowed and sidetracked by the American domestic politics (the Watergate scandal), but continued under the Jimmy Carter administration, with one slight change. The "tilting" game under Kissinger was changed into a "card playing" game under Zbigniew Brzezinski, the National Security Advisor to President Carter. Brzezinski accepted the three premises of Kissinger, despite his verbal assertions to the contrary. The most obvious difference was his purported departure from Kissinger's "supergame" in his simultaneous attention to the "rising crescendo" of the countries in the southern arc. The Kissingerian Supergame was not to be abandoned, so much as to be played within a larger, truly global, context.[62]

---

[61] Hsiung, see note 54, pp. 119–122.

[62] Ibid., pp. 126–128.

In retrospect, neither under President Carter, nor later administrations, was there any significantly different architecture of U.S. foreign policy, deviating from the one laid down by the Nixon-Kissinger team. The "China card" game, begun under the Carter Administration, continued and lasted until the Reagan administration, which coincided with the ascension to power of Mikhail Gorbachev in the Soviet Union. Gorbachev's visit to Washington to sign the Intermediate Nuclear Force Treaty (INF) with Reagan in 1997 symbolized a return to normalcy in United States–Soviet relations, and the beginning of the end of the Cold War. But, Gorbachev's Glasnost policy and attempted reform unexpectedly brought down the Communist Party of the Soviet Union's (CPSU) monopoly of power, and the subsequent demise of the Soviet Union.

The importance for our concern here is that, with the removal of the Soviet threat, the value of the "China card" has also vanished. Hence, the post-Cold War Sino–U.S. relations have been drifting almost aimlessly, until the deterioration into the Trump-era contest, fraught with the danger of a Thucydides Trap, which was abetted by China's phenomenal re-rise.

But the U.S. practice of using China to balance against the Soviet Union, in retrospect, seemed to have set an example for what President Trump attempted to do, in 2017, in making use of China's influence as a diplomatic tool for taming a nuclear ambitious North Korea. In the circumstances, so long as the Korean peninsula crisis continues, the United States–China contest may witness a temporary respite, as we will explain in Chapter 6.

Chapter

6

The U.S.–China Contest (I): A Clash of Visions and the Chain of Escalatory Reactions

In order to fully comprehend the origins and implications of the gathering storm over the post-2010 U.S.–China contest, we need to tackle two totally different ways of interpreting the perceived reality, between Washington and Beijing. Here, let us recall an adage made famous by Immanuel Kant, that the facts we perceive may not be the same as the facts-in-themselves. The word "vision" here refers, specifically, to the idiosyncratic perception of the facts, respectively from the U.S. and the Chinese standpoints. This point merits special attention because decision makers react only to their perceived reality, as exists in their vision, not to the true reality, the facts-in-themselves.

By "clash of visions," I am referring to the misreading of each other's intentions based on the varied perceptions between U.S. and Chinese decision makers, potentially driving them into an escalatory spiral.

The China–U.S. clash of visions may or may not end in a Peloponnesian-type war, fulfilling the parable of the Thucydides Trap.[1] The ultimate outcome, however, depends on whether the distorted perceptions can be duly corrected to jive with the facts-in-themselves. This is not entirely wishful thinking, but is supported by a real example of how such a change of heart can come about when the real truth is driven home to confound and expel the clouds of an earlier misimpression. The case in point is related to a pledge by candidate Donald Trump, made on his 2016 campaign trail, that if elected, he would on his first day in office declare China a currency manipulator. After his inauguration, he did not do as promised. During one of the White House meetings he hosted for top business leaders, President Trump raised the question to Jamie Dimon, CEO of JPMorgan Chase, on whether the Chinese were manipulating their currency. As the *New York Times* reported, quoting two persons who were also present, Mr. Dimon replied: "No, Mr. President, they are not. I think they're trying to be responsible."[2] This answer not only agreed with the advice of Trump's staff and Cabinet that he should abandon his campaign pledge, but also had support in an International Monetary Fund (IMF) finding, as reported by Bloomberg News, that the Chinese did not manipulate their *yuan* after 2007.[3] Thereafter, President Trump reversed himself on his campaign trail accusation of the Chinese being currency manipulators.

After everything has been said, it remains true, nevertheless, that the clash of visions on other vital issues, if not rectified in time, may

[1] "Thucydides Trap" is named after the great ancient Greek historian, Thucydides, who studied the Peloponnesian War, and explained, "the rise of Athens and the fear this instilled in Sparta that made war inevitable."

[2] "Giving Advice, Business Titans Feel at Home in White House," *New York Times*, April 30, 2017, 1.

[3] William Pesek, "Stop Calling China a Currency Manipulator," *Bloomberg News*, May 28, 2015, in which he quoted the IMF's Christine Lagarde as saying China's currency was no longer undervalued. "The yuan," he added, "can't gain status as a global currency reserve if China is thought to be manipulating its value. So who should we believe, the head of the International Monetary Fund or the U.S. Treasury Secretary?"

still have consequential effects on the fate of the U.S.–China contest. Another such element that may have a bearing on the outcome of the contest is the strategy consciously adopted by decision makers in Washington and Beijing, for managing their competition and conflict (more on this in the next chapter).

The ongoing unease and tensions reflective of the mutual distrust between a suspicious and defensive U.S. superpower and a rising China perceived to be on an "assertive" course resulted from a clash of visions, as defined earlier. Unfortunately, this is a point that has not been studied in depth; and we almost have to start from scratch. For one thing, we can draw on the relevant lessons that can be gleaned from the sketches of U.S.–China relations, including the United States' China policy, which we examined in the previous chapter. On that basis, we hope to be able to cobble together a U.S. vision on the unstoppable rise of China and the challenge it poses to the United States. As to the Chinese vision, on the other hand, we can likewise draw on the outlines of China's experience narrated in the last chapter. When called for, we will try to tap additional data that are relevant for an adequate appreciation of China's vision, including a self-image on its own rerise. Of course, how the rerising China will behave on the international scene will, for a large part, depend on its self-image, which in part will also be shaped by its perception of how its own rerise is greeted by the major actors on the world stage.

The U.S. Vision on China's Rise

Most people, including many pundits as well, are either not aware of, or not serious about, the significance of the fact that China's current rise is its second ascent on a path of national rejuvenation. One notable exception, however, is Henry Kissinger, who wrote in his 2011 book: "China produced a greater share of total world GDP than any Western society in 18 of the last 20 centuries. As late as 1820, it produced over 30% of world GDP — an amount exceeding the GDP of Western Europe, Eastern Europe, and the United States combined."[4]

[4] Henry Kissinger, *On China* (New York: The Penguin Press, 2011), pp. 11–12.

Given this rich knowledge, Kissinger was concerned that other political commentators, following their instinct, might succumb to the line of thinking reminiscent of Eyre Crowe, a past senior official in the British Foreign Office. In a 1907 report, Crowe foresaw that Germany's rise, *in itself*, regardless of its intentions, would be an operative threat to Britain. Kissinger was worried that those who follow Crowe's intuition may just see China's "rise" *per se* — "whatever China's intentions" — as being "incompatible with America's position in the Pacific and by extension the world."[5]

"The American debate," Kissinger continued, "adds an ideological challenge to Crowe's balance-of-power approach." In other words, to neoconservatives, nondemocratic societies like the PRC "are inherently precarious and prone to the *exercise of force*." And, "in these conceptions," he added "regime change is the ultimate goal of American foreign policy in dealing with nondemocratic societies; and peace with China is less a matter of strategy than of *change in Chinese governance*" (emphasis added).[6]

Thus seen, the initiative in the "exercise of force," may conversely be rooted in the American policy toward China, so long as it is considered to be a "nondemocratic society" to be removed by external intervention, if necessary, for the sake of peace, notwithstanding China's intentions, including its refusal to resort to the offensive use of force. Hence, Kissinger went on to paraphrase a pessimistic lament from a book called *China Dream* by Colonel Liu Mingfu in China: No matter how much China commits itself to a "peaceful rise," conflict is inherent in U.S.–China relations. The relationship between China and the United States will be, in Liu's words, a "marathon contest" and "duel of the century."[7]

Kissinger's scary rendition of the U.S. vision with regard to the (perceived) challenge arising from China's rise can actually find corroboration in the logic inherent in the evolution of U.S.–China policy

---

[5] Ibid., p. 520.

[6] Ibid.

[7] Ibid., p. 521.

we discussed in the previous chapter, as is briefly summarized below for the reader's convenience.

Past U.S.–China Policy Initiatives: and Current U.S. Vision on China's Rise

We have seen that the image of China, in its evolving relations with the United States since the 19th century, has undergone several changes from its earliest attraction as an "illimitable" market place, then as an "object" in U.S. policy (as under the U.S. Open Door policy and the Nine-Power Treaty), to a wartime ally fighting a common enemy in the Pacific War (after Pearl Harbor), an expected post–World War II (WWII) stabilizer in Asia (watching over a potentially resurgent Japan) and a fence against the Soviet Heartland Power (in FDR's Rimland strategy scenario), then an ideologically defined target for containment (after the Communist rise to power in China in 1949), and to a potential partner (in U.S. balancing against the Soviet Union) as well as a player in a triadic nuclear deterrence match in the Kissingerian "tilting" game (during the Nixon administration), which morphed into a "card playing" game in Brezezinski's maneuverings (under President Carter), that culminated in the normalization of U.S.–China relations in 1979.

In all these periods, China was never really an equal entity in terms of power, either in reality or in U.S. perception. In America's "tilting" and "card playing" games in the 1970s, a strategic premise, or implicit requirement, was that China be powerful enough as a counterweight in the balancing game against the Soviet Union, but not so powerful as to threaten the United States itself. Another premise was that only a continuing Soviet threat would justify the value of China as a strategic partner that merits the special U.S. accommodations to it.

Now, by the second decade of the 21st century, both these premises were rendered nonexistent by the change of time. While the Cold War had ended with the collapse of Soviet power by 1990, a rising China has edged forward in power to a position perceived to be challenging to the United States, at least economically, if not yet militarily.

Nevertheless, it is scary that China's economic output has registered a 20-fold increase since the late 1970s. Thus, the general impressions of a surging U.S.–China contest, with tensions radiating through the Pacific region, potentially upsetting the global order built on U.S.-made rules since the end of WWII, were no longer a figment of imagination, but perceived to be a well-founded reality. That crystallized in the "China threat" scare which underscores the current U.S. contest with China.

It remains true that reactions of the decision makers are shaped, more often than not, by their respective perceptions, which we described as the clashing "visions" between Washington and Beijing. Likewise, whether a resolution of the tensions can be found, so that the two great powers will learn to live in peace, will depend on whether the clash in vision can be effectively rectified in time. The answer, hopefully, will become clearer after we examine China's "vision" on its own rerise and, moreover, on how its reemergence from over a century of decline and disgrace is being greeted, undeniably with suspicion and distrust across the Pacific Ocean.

The Chinese Vision on Its Own Rerise and How It is Greeted by the United States

It is much harder to depict the Chinese vision with regard to world affairs, including their relations with the United States, because of the much longer Chinese history in which their experiences with the outside world in different periods were very varied. If broad generalizations can be made, their current vision of world affairs is heavily influenced by their very different experiences from two separate periods in history: (a) the period that was coextensive with the so-called "Tribute System" (roughly 1368 through 1840), during which China was the suzerain (the "central kingdom") surrounded by a group of "vassal" states that at regular intervals sent their envoys to China bearing "tributes," by which the system got its name; and (b) the second period that comprised the one and a half centuries (beginning from 1840) when China's fortunes were down, often being at the mercy of the Western colonial/imperialistic powers (and jingoistic

Japan) that accounted for the encroachments and violations of its sovereignty (and dignity).

We will be interested to see what effects these varied experiences have wrought on China's psyche (to the extent assessable) and behavioral proclivities during its current rerise. Since the latter period is more easily explicable, we will begin with China's encounters with the predatory foreign powers during the post-1840 era.

The Effects of China's Experience in Dealing with Foreign Powers Since the 1840 Opium War

As we have noted in the last chapter, China's first rise ended in 1820, more than a millennium after it had begun. Although Manchu China's decline was engendered by a combination of both domestic problems and encroachments by foreign powers, the most crushing blow, without doubt, was delivered by the two Opium Wars and what they brought in their aftermath. In short, they resulted from the British attempt to open the China market for the opium grown in their Indian colony. In this, the unmatched British naval might was thrown fully behind the massive commercial interests in pushing the opium down the collective throat of the Chinese. After its defeat, China had to sign unequal treaties, in 1842 and again in 1858, legalizing the Opium trade, among other concessions, which included the cession of Hong Kong. They set an example for more unequal treaties exacted by other foreign powers. The massive opium imports into China, consequentially, ruined both the Chinese economy and the physical health of the Chinese elites (including many among the imperial family), among the rest of the nation. That hastened the pace of Manchu China's decline, until its downfall in 1911. Other European powers (and Japan), seizing their opportunities to exploit the weakening and dying empire, swooped down *en mass*, in the second half of the 19th century, to prey on the Chinese in their moment of weakness and distress. All together, nine foreign countries had garnered either hefty concessions or spheres of influence in various parts of China. The territories snatched away by the powers from China totaled 2.5 million square miles, or 50 times the size of New

York state. Russia, alone, annexed the Ili region along the border in northwest China (later legalized by treaty) and then acquired huge tracts of land north of the Amur River and east of the Ussuri River. The latter covered an area that added up to 11 times the size of New York state. All these losses were sealed by unequal treaties China was forced to sign at gun point.[8]

The Open Door policy and the Nine-Power Treaty of 1922, cultivated and sponsored by the United States with good wishes, did little to help shore up, much less to reverse, the falling fortunes of a helpless China at the time.

David Scott, among others, considers China's modern period of encounter with the West, 1840 through 1949, as the *Century of Humiliation*. During this time, China fell from "Middle Kingdom" preeminence to a position in the international system that remained an enigmatic one: too strong to be taken over as a colony, yet not strong enough to shape its own destiny.[9] Franklin Houn thinks that the Chinese Communist Party (CCP) under Mao Zedong rode the anti-imperialist tide in a populist drive to "conquer power" in China.[10] In fact, Mao himself had confirmed that one of the goals of the CCP revolution was the expurgation of the "imperialist" inroads in China; and he expressed confidence that whoever could lead in the nation's anti-imperialist struggle would win the mandate to rule China and free it from foreign domination.[11]

---

[8] James C. Hsiung, *China into Its Second Rise* (Singapore: World Scientific, 2012), 75f. For a study of the unequal treaties China had to sign during the 19th century, see William L. Tung, *China and the Foreign Powers* (Dobbs Ferry, NY: Oceana Publications, 1970).

[9] David Scott, *China and the International System, 1840–1949: Power, Presence, and Perceptions in a Century of Humiliations* (Albany, NY: SUNY Press, 2008).

[10] Franklin Houn, *A Short History of Chinese Communism* (Englewood, NJ: Prentice-Hall, 1973).

[11] Mao Zedong, "Lun xin minzhu zhuyi [On New Democracy]," *Mao Zedong sixjang xuanji [Selected Works of Mao Zedong]*, vol. 3: 535f. In the original, Mao added to the anti-imperialist cause a second, but no less important cause, namely: the "fan fengiian" struggle, which has been consistently mistranslated as "anti-feudal" cause. The correct translation should be "anti-backward."

A summing up. Let us pause now to see if we can generalize from the Chinese experience during this so-called century of humiliation and arrive at a profile of what modern-day China, during its second rise, is likely to do in its foreign policy and international behavior. I think it is safe to conclude that China is most likely to live out its frustrations with two previous predators, namely: Western (and Japanese) "imperialism" and Stalinist-type chauvinism. It is likely to rise to the call for international (social) justice.[12] And it will stand in opposition to the Western notion of social Darwinism, which provided the justification for the "Whiteman's Burden," used (mostly by the British) as a fig leaf to over up past colonialist and imperialist licentiousness.

I might add that in China's rerising today, if there is any grudge it holds for past foreign predators, the United States is decidedly not among them, as it was the author of the Nine-Power Treaty of 1922 that sought to internationalize the American Open Door policy, to save a dying Manchu China from the danger of partition at the hands of European powers (plus Japan), a feat that we noted in Chapter 2.

Even toward Britain, despite the ferocious tragedy the British Opium Wars brought to the Chinese, as noted before, China's magnanimity and forgiveness, a virtue taught by Confucius, was amply on display during President Xi Jinping's four-day visit to London in October 2015. In his address at the Buckingham Palace banquet given in his honor, he began with words of atonement in Chinese, which implored in effect: "Bygones should only fade in memory, yielding to a new page of history in which we in China are prepared to build with the United Kingdom a relationship of healthy interdependence and shared interests." One wonders how many in the United Kingdom fully understood and appreciated his generous

[12] During the drafting stage of the U.N. Charter, before and during the 1945 UNCIO conference in San Francisco, the first mention of "justice" in the final U.N. Charter (Art. 2(3)) was the result of an amendment to the original Dumbarton Oaks draft, at the insistence of China (ROC). James C. Hsiung, see note 8, p. 273. In the cases in which it canceled (forgave) the debts owed by LDC borrowers, China was showing its empathy in generous attempts to remedy instances of "social injustice." Ibid., p. 250.

words "bygones should only fade in memory." In her response, the Queen said this was a "very special year for our bilateral relationship." The British press noted that "Xi's visit came amid job losses in the UK steel sector, with cheap Chinese imports among factors being blamed."[13] The tone made it sound that the British, not the Chinese, were being magnanimous and forgiving.

Effects of China's experience from the Tribute System's network of international relations (IR) (1368–1820), with its own rules of the game.

David Kang did a study of the patterns of IR in these nearly five centuries of the Chinese Tribute System, calling it "East Asia before the West." In a comparison with the Westphalia system of States, he found two distinct features in the Tribute System. First, there were by far fewer instances of war; and in the five centuries he studied, there were only two (indigenous) international wars, of which China started one, not counting the wars brought by the European powers. Second, the states in the Tribute System were nominally unequal, but in fact equal, as they fell into a hierarchy headed by China in a (mostly nominal) suzerain–vassal relationship.[14]

The second difference in comparison with the Westphalia system holds much greater theoretical significance than meets the eye. In the mainstream IR theory developed by the Neorealists, the Westphalia system of states is defined by its characteristic premise of ***anarchy***, denoting the absence of a superior authority (such as a world government would symbolize) over and above the nation-states that make up the system. From this anarchic premise, everything else flows into being, such as sovereign coequality of states, balance of power as a necessary self-help tool to ensure national security, and so on. A foremost concern of Neorealist IR theory, therefore, is the perils of unbalanced power, whoever wields it, in the anarchic system.[15] Balance of

---

[13] "Xi Jinping Visit: UK-China Ties 'Will Be lifted to New Height'," *BBC News*, October 20, 2015.

[14] David Kang, *East Asia Before the West: Five Centuries of Trade and Tribute* (New York: Columbia University Press, 2010).

[15] Kenneth N. Waltz, *Theory of International Politics* (Reading, MA: Addison-Wesley Publishing, 1979).

power, a necessary statecraft to contain the perils of unbalanced power, requires constant shifting coalitions, in accordance with the changing structure of power distribution over time. It may require the use of force to meet the challenge of the wielder (either a State or a coalition of States) of threatening force. Hence, the much higher incidence of wars in the Westphalia system. And, a central feature in this anarchic system is that the lesser states, especially when led by a rising power, are expected to band together to balance the existing hegemon, whose power poses a threat to every other State.

In the alternative Tribute System model, by contrast, a central feature of the game is bandwagoning by the secondary states, rather than balancing against the "central state," a position occupied by China (zhongguo, 中國, literally, the central kingdom or state). "Built on a mix of legitimate authority and material power," Kang notes, "the tribute system provided a normative social order that also contained credible commitments by China not to exploit secondary states that accepted its [moral] authority."[16]

The key to understanding this Tribute System and how it worked is that it was a typical model characterized by hierarchy, rather than anarchy. To the extent that the central state has no territorial ambitions, and when there exists a method for resolving conflicts, Kang finds, the model shows that all nations in the system can find equilibrium that involves acquiescence to the dominant state. From this acquiescence, the secondary states are able to maintain their autonomy and de facto equality while enjoying the stability and other benefits the hierarchical system bestows. Hence, bandwagoning by secondary states is their optimal choice in a steep hierarchy like the Tributary System.[17]

I hasten to add that the Chinese view of hierarchy was not a one-way street; and it allowed for China's acceptance of an inferior status for itself in the event of an inverse hierarchy. This did not just exist in theory, but in real historical periods when China was in a less powerful position vis-à-vis a more powerful foreign state, such as the

---

[16] Kang, *East Asia before the West*, p. 2.

[17] Ibid., pp. 8–12.

Jin (or Chin, 金) during the Southern Sung (Song) dynasty (1127–1259). To make peace in 1138 with the Jin (a state founded by the Tungusic people, also known as Nuchen, in the Sungari basin in Manchuria, today's northeast China), the founder of the Chinese Southern Sung Dynasty even accepted the status of a "vassal" (chen, 臣) for himself. The Southern Sung emperors sent to their powerful northern neighbor annual presents of large amounts and value, nominally as a kind of economic aid, but actually as a tribute in reverse flow.[18]

These little-known episodes are enough to indicate that in the (past) Sinocentric hierarchy of East Asian IR, the suzerain–vassal (patron–client) relationship was at times reversible, although for the most part Chinese primacy was the norm. After the arrival of Western powers, and especially after China's defeat in the Opium War of 1840, the hierarchy was permanently reversed, and the Chinese learned to live with the reversal. The decisive part, which most analysts have missed, is whether China is politically "in" the world's existing system. Maoist China, despite its weakness and an economy mostly in disarray, revolted against the U.S. hegemony precisely because the Beijing regime was excluded from the international system by dint of the United States' nonrecognition, a policy that most of its allies followed — until 1979, or seven years following Nixon's ice-breaking visit in 1972.

In contrast to the Maoist period, China is now very much "in" the Westphalia system, albeit an inverse hierarchical system with the United States at its head. Finding itself in a position comparable to the secondary states in the Tribute System of yore, Beijing has followed the rules of the game borne of the past hierarchical (Tribune) system and has, accordingly, been playing a bandwagoning role vis-à-vis the U.S. hegemon. That is the reality, or facts-in-themselves. But, unfortunately, it is not the perception of the U.S. government, which is aided by the theorizing of the Neorealist IR experts.

---

[18]YANG Lien-sheng, "Historical Notes on the Chinese World Order," in John K. Fairbank, ed., *The Chinese World Order: Traditional Chinese Foreign Relations* (Cambridge, MA: Harvard University Press, 1968), 20ff.

Neorealist IR theory, in fact, predicted that in the post–Cold War world, after the Soviet demise, a rising power like China would seek to balance the unipolar power of the United States. In fact, Kenneth Waltz in 2000 had predicted that even before the (re)rising China arrives, the other secondary states, such as Japan, European Union (EU), and Russia will either singularly or in concert rise to balance the U.S. hegemony.[19] Now well into the third decade of the post–Cold War era, none of these secondary states has even showed an interest, much less taken action, to counterbalance the U.S. hegemonic power. As Peter Van Ness poignantly points out, the reason is that States today live in a hierarchical, rather than anarchic, system.[20] I would add that there is plenty of evidence that China has been bandwagoning to the U.S. hegemon in the existing inverse hierarchical system. The following three select cases should suffice to illustrate this very point.[21]

North Korea

The first such case has to do with the dealings with North Korea, or Democratic People's Republic of Korea (DPRK). In October 2002, North Korea admitted that it was pursuing a covert nuclear weapons program. Faced with this DPRK nuclear ambition, the United States, in conjunction with South Korea and Japan, had tried to use the "carrots" of a 1994 agreement, to induce Pyonyang to freeze its nuclear program, in exchange for energy aid and a promise to provide it with two light-water nuclear reactors, but to no avail. In late 2003, President George W. Bush turned to the Chinese for help, asking them to use their immense influence to bring North Korea to the negotiating table (*New York Times*, October 19, 2003, p. 6). If it

[19] Kenneth N. Walatz, "Structural Realism After the Cold War," *International Security*, vol. 25, no. 1: 5–41.

[20] Peter Van Ness, "Hegemony, Not Anarchy: Why China and Japan Are Not Balancing against U.S. Unipolar Power," *International Relations of the Asia Pacific* (Tokyo), vol. 2, no.1: 131–150.

[21] In this discussion, I am relying on my *China into Its Second Rise*, see note 8, pp. 252–257.

were Stalin, faced with the same U.S.–DPRK stand-off, he probably would have manipulated the erratic and swashbuckling North Korea as a leverage to strengthen his hand in his country's brutal rivalry with Washington. But, complying with the wishes of Uncle Sam, Beijing' leader, Hu Jintao, brokered the Six-Party talks, held in Beijing, as a way to rein in the North Koreans. Besides China, United States, and DPRK, three others including South Korea, Japan, and Russia also attended. Five rounds of talks were held from 2004 to 2007, but produced little progress. The Chinese applied heat by ordering sanctions, such as cutting off food supplies and fuel, on both of which North Korea was heavily dependent on China, and also by cutting off North Korea's only banking links with the outside world via Macao. That, finally, did the trick. A breakthrough came on February 13, 2007, when the Talks ended with the adoption of a document on the specific steps to be taken toward the denuclearization of the Korean Peninsula. North Korea agreed to shut down and seal its Yongbyon nuclear facility, and to invite back inspectors from the International Atomic Energy Agency (IAEA) to conduct all necessary monitoring and verifications. The parties agreed to the provision of emergency energy assistance to DPRK. They also agreed to resume the Six-Party Talks in five months. Another side-agreement, which was more enticing for the North Koreans, was that the United States would meet with DPRK representatives in direct bilateral talks later in New York.[22] Although North Korea later reneged on its commitment toward cessation of its nuclear program, which happened only after it had initially dismantled its Yongbyon facility. And, more important, the reneging came after the United States abruptly discontinued the direct dialogue with DPRK representatives after the first round of meeting in New York. The North not only resumed its missile and nuclear testing, but made such a fanfare of them as if it was afraid the outside world (the United States) would not know about these tests. This explosive behavior merely serves to confirm a political motive of trying to mount pressures on Washington for the resumption of the

[22] "Six-Party Talks End with Joint Statement," *China News Service*, October 13, 2007.

direct DPRK–U.S. talks. The ultimate goal North Korea hopes to accomplish from the direct talks was a negotiated peace treaty, to legally terminate the status of belligerency, over 60 years after the 1953 Armistice Agreement ended the hostilities, but not the state of war. What really matters in the broad context is that the case unmistakably demonstrated China's willingness and efforts to help rein in the North Koreans in compliance with U.S. wishes, in ways that Stalin would never have agreed to do. Nor would any foreign government that was bent on counterbalancing the hegemonic power of the United States. To bring things up to date, when President Trump asked the Chinese to intercede again in the face of the renewed tension between Washington and Pyongyang, in 2017, there was little they could do to help, unless Trump would agree to resume the direct talks between the United States and the North.[23]

Iran

Our second example concerns China's management of its delicate relations with Iran in the latter's conflict with the United States. Iran has never caused security concerns for China because of the geographical distance. Instead, there is a long tradition of cooperation between the two countries dating back many centuries, during which ancient empires of the two lands were connected via the Silk Road. For years since the 1980s, China's "arms for oil" policy brought it into a very close relationship with Iran, which was desperately in need of an arms replenishment following the Iran–Iraq War. Iran thus was the best market for Chinese arms exports and, in return, it also became the third most important oil supplier for China's insatiable needs. This close relationship presented what became known as China's "Persian Gulf dilemma" when the United States adopted the Iran-Libya Sanctions Act (ILSA) in 1996, and imposed sanctions on

[23] With this in view, it was scarcely coincidental that Trump expressed his willingness (in fact, it was his "honor") to meet with Kim Jong-un himself at the appropriate time.

Iran. This dilemma, according to John Garver,[24] "requires China to balance a major interest in maintaining comity with the United States against its interests in building cooperative ties to important (Persian) Gulf countries — including those, like the Islamic Republic [of Iran], in policy conflict with Washington." China's leaders have been careful not to let their country's ties with Iran be perceived in Washington as a direct challenge to America's hegemonic position.[25] Eventually, this caution led to China's support for the U.S.-sought resolution in the U.N. Security Council authorizing sanctions on Iran (UNSC Res. 1929, adopted on June 9, 2010). Media reports, however, drummed up a juicy (but untrue) story about why China turned around to vote for the resolution, alleging a U.S.–Saudi collaboration to "wean China off Iranian oil" by increasing Saudi oil supplies, at the U.S. behest.[26] All alleged that under heavy U.S. pressures, the Saudis had provided assurances to China that it could count on Saudi oil supplies to make up for the slack in the event Iranian oil supplies should be cut off. The only condition, they added, was that China must take tangible actions to restrain Iran's nuclear ambitions.

These media reports, on closer examination, are not credible for a number of reasons: First, between China and the United States, Saudi Arabia has a much closer relationship with the former. As the *New York Times* (April 20, 2011) pointed out, U.S. support for Israel has created friction with Saudi Arabia, quoting a view from Prince Irki al-Faisal, a former Saudi ambassador to the United States and brother of the foreign minister, Prince Saud al-Faisal. By comparison, he added, "with China, there is less baggage, there are easier routes to mutual benefit." Ever since 1999, the Saudi Kingdom has been

---

[24] John Garver, *China and Iran: Ancient Partners in the Post-Imperial World* (Seattle, WA: University of Washington Press, 2006).

[25] Mahnaz Zhirinejad, "Implication of New World Order on China's Energy Policy Towards Iran," *Asia-Pacific Journal of Social Sciences* Special Issue No. 1 (December 2010): 119.

[26] For example, the Reuters wire service carried a by-lined story by Melanie Lee to that effect, on May 2, 2011, crediting WikiLeaks for its source. The Eurasia Information Network also carried a similar story by Sekiyama Takashi, dated December 6, 2010, under the headlines: "Why China Backed the Iran Sanctions."

forging ever closer ties with China, and if the Chinese should need the assurances, they could have gotten them directly from the Saudis, without going through any go-between, not in the least the United States. Second, contrary to the assumption of these media reports, Saudi Arabia is not China's no.1 supplier of oil, having been overtaken by Angola since 2007. At the end of 2008, Angola, which had been negotiating for years with the IMF for a loan, informed the latter's officials that China had just granted to Angola a low-interest $2 billion loan and, therefore, an IMF loan would no longer be needed. Considering the close ties between China and Angola, one might question: In view of the strained U.S.–Saudi relations, why could not the United States have collaborated with the Angolans if oil supply assurances were necessary to "wean the Chinese off the Iranian oil"? Thirdly, since China could have directly obtained the same assurances from Angola, or Saudi Arabia, and, in addition, since it has its own heavy investments in oil projects in Africa (and 30% of China's oil needs come from Africa as a whole), the Chinese decidedly would not feel so much in U.S. debt — even if these media reports were true — so as to drastically change their country's vote — not to cast its veto — in the U.N. Security Council just to "repay" Washington for what it allegedly had done in getting them the (fictitious) Saudi assurances. The bottom line here is that China's final decision to support the resolution, as far as I know, was out of considerations by Beijing not to jeopardize its overall relations with Washington. Thus, another example of bandwagoning.

Libya

Still another example of China's bandwagoning to the United States concerned what to do about Libya. As the "Jasmine Revolution" fever spread in North Africa, it caught on in Libya in February 2011. Throngs of people took to the streets, demanding the ouster of Col. Muammar Qaddafi, who had kept power for 41 years with what the *Economist* (February 26, 2011, p. 25) called his "violently capricious rule." The unrest swarmed from Tripoli, the national capital, swiftly to Benghazi, the second largest city. Like in Tripoli, where gangs of soldiers and snipers had spread terror on the demonstrators, in Benghazi, too, the troops launched a brutal crackdown on protestors. Former Libyan ambassador to the United States, Ali Aujali, who backed the rebels, appealed for immediate help from the West. Unconfirmed reports said that funds were released from Libyan government assets frozen in American banks to the rebels fighting Qaddafi, as bloodshed intensified. After Secretary of State Hillary Clinton made a trip to France in early March, to meet with European leaders on the next steps for addressing the civil war in Libya, the United States under the Obama Administration began to shift its tone in support of a resolution to be adopted by the U.N. Security Council to authorize, nominally, a "no-fly" zone to aid Libyan rebels. The resolution (UNSC 1973) was adopted by the Security Council on March 10, 2011, with a 10–0 vote with five abstentions, including China and Russia, either of which wields a veto on the Council.

China, due to its own bitter experience with external interventions in its century of humiliation since 1840, was opposed to the use of force or coercion against any country, not just Qaddafi's Libya. Even though the UNSC Resolution nominally called for "all necessary measures," including a "no-fly" zone, to protect civilians from attacks by forces led by Qaddafi, from the Chinese point of view, it had loopholes that could be exploited by North Atlantic Treaty Organization (NATO) forces to launch strikes on Qaddafi's air defenses. But, in the end, China abstained, rather than casting a veto against the Resolution. To fully grasp the magnitude of this self-restraint, one would have to consider two things that might have crossed the minds of the Chinese leaders, one hypothetical and one probable. The first is what would have happened in a similar situation during the U.S.–Soviet rivalry in the Cold War. The Soviet Union would surely have vetoed a resolution like the one introduced in the Security Council and backed by the United States and its NATO allies. Now that China has replaced the Soviet Union as the power that most people think is in a position to challenge the United States on who has the final say on an international issue like Libya's unrest. But, the fact is that China chose not to veto the resolution. The other item that must have seized the attention of the Chinese decision makers is that the Libyan issue was not just what it appeared to be, but involved a hidden U.S. rivalry with China in Africa, a region that supplies 30% of the oil imports of China. By March 2011, according to Chinese Ministry of Trade, 75 major Chinese companies were operating in Libya and they had concluded $18 billion in contracts. NATO operations in Libya of the kind authorized by the Security Council would leave these Chinese interests with potential gigantic losses. It is not surprising that some media reports alleged that Washington was "using NATO as a proxy conflict with China in Libya."[27] Be that as it may, the Chinese stoically skewed to the United States and decided not to cast a veto against the U.S.-backed resolution in the Security Council, lest it be taken as an affront to thwart U.S. wishes. As if to blunt possible criticisms that China was being too obsequious to U.S. wishes, it cited an earlier Arab League statement in support of the "no-fly" zone as a reason for the Chinese abstention on the vote.

In doing so, China was unwittingly displaying both self-confidence and undue trust in NATO. It was self-confident that its own economic interests and political weight in Africa would not be shaken by the effects of such sanctions as UNSC Resolution 1973 would bring. China knew it had acquired firm political weight in Africa (including Libya), as it did not subject African political leaders to harangues about human rights. On a grassroots level, again unlike the United States and West European nations, China, along with its business interests, was building infrastructure, such as roads, railways, and schools, which was much appreciated by the local populace. In addition to Angola, it has extended low-interest loans, totaling billions of dollars, to African countries such as Chad, Nigeria, Sudan, Ethiopia, and Uganda, after they had been turned away by the IMF.[28] But, in deciding against a veto, China also showed too much trust in the likelihood that NATO would faithfully implement UNSC Resolution 1973. When later it turned out that NATO's (unauthorized) bombings had killed or

---

[27] "A World Future Online report," retrieved, http://oilprice.com/Geo-Politics/international/Is-NATO-Being-Used-by-Washington-in-Libya-to-Hurt-Chinese.
[28] Ibid.

wounded scores of civilians they were supposed to protect against Qaddafi's forces, China could only "urge" a quick end to air strikes in Libya. In this, it was promptly joined by Brazil, Russia, and India, the other three of the BRIC nations (*New York Times*, 22 March, 2011). All four had abstained on the vote, although only China and Russia had a veto power on the Security Council.

Conclusion

In sum, we can conclude by recognizing that the rerising China has shown a consistent pattern of bandwagoning to the United States, the reigning superpower, during the post–Cold War period that coincided with its own rerise. This bandwagoning behavior confirms a pattern in the former (East Asian) tribute system under Chinese primacy (1368–1840), in which secondary states bandwagoned to the dominant power, rather than balancing against it, as noted before. In this light, although the Chinese vision differs from the American vision, the current bilateral tensions are not the result of what Neorealist IR theory predicts about a Thucydides Trap, brought on by a rising China in competition with the hegemonic power of the United States.

What Precipitated the Post-2010 U.S.–China Contest?

The first round of the "clash of visions" game witnessed a clash between the U.S. vision, on the one hand, that greeted the rise of China with alarm, and, on the other hand, a Chinese vision that placed itself in the position of a secondary state in a hierarchical system, bearing resemblance to the past Tribute System, except with the power ratio in reverse. But, after playing out the bandwagoning role as befitting a secondary state in a hierarchical system recalling the Tribute system familiar to it, China found that it failed to receive even goodwill in return. Not only that, it only met with suspicion, and worse. As noted in Chapter 1, the instigating pep talk given by Secretary Hillary Clinton to the ASEAN regional forum in July 2010 served to foster renewed confrontations with China in the South China Sea (SCS) by the Philippines and later by Vietnam, both in

2011. A spillover effect, in retaliation, was China's seizure of control of the previously unpopulated Scarborough Reef, in 2012, during a stand-off with Philippine maritime vessels, despite agreeing to a mutual withdrawal brokered by Washington. And, with the legal help from Washington,[29] the Philippines even took China to an arbitral joust before a Permanent Court of Arbitration (PCA) tribunal in 2013, as we discussed in Chapter 4. In January 2012, the Obama administration issued a New Defense Guideline, which announced his "Pivot to Asia" policy. Although described as a "rebalancing" policy in Asia, the "Pivot" initiative was in fact aimed at containing China by mobilizing Southeast Asian nations, as noted in Chapter 1. In an atmosphere where it felt being caved in from all sides on issues related to the SCS, ranging from the U.S. rebuke and naval surveillance under the pretext of protecting the freedom of navigation, to the renewed but heightened counterclaim brawls from Vietnam and the Philippines among ASEAN nations, China reacted with a program of building artificial islands out of reefs and other features in SCS. But, this move, which had been prompted by China's attempt to reassert its claims in the SCS, to counter the renewed assertiveness of Vietnam and the Philippines, in turn, received strong objection from the U.S. side in a counterreaction that included more vociferous rebukes and stepped-up naval patrolling in the SCS. Thus, the post-2010 U.S.–China contest became a fixed feature as a result.

Perception Gap, Reaction, Counterreaction, and Counter to Counterreaction, *ad infinitum*

We all know it takes two to tango. And, in any bilateral contest, escalation means a progression from one side's action (let us call it "action-1"), provoking the other side's reaction, which in turn evokes a counterreaction, which then elicits a counter to the counterreaction, *ad infinitum*. But in the escalation of the post-2010 U.S.–China

[29] In the Philippines' arbitral complaint against China, it was ably aided by the expert legal counsel of Lawrence H. Martin, Esq., from the famous Foley Hoag law firm in Washington, DC.

face-off, the question is: Which party, after all, is responsible for the crucial "action-1" that started the chain of reactions and counterreactions? In trying to fix the responsibility, bystander analysts invariably encounter two difficulties. One is the perception gap between the parties, and the other is the impulse by either contending party to impute the blame to the other side. The difficulty is made more acute by the fact that the English-speaking spectators are treated to an abundance of Western media reports as well as official U.S. assertions that is not equally found from the Chinese side. And, Beijing's media-shy problem — nay, deliberate refusal to comment in response — is well known, as Paul Denlinger has cogently observed.[30]

Even among bystander analysts, there is also a perceptual problem that is bound to result in varied conclusions, drawn from the same facts, but viewed from different angles. For example, on the question as to which country was responsible for what we have called "action-1" earlier, I know of two distinctly opposing views among competent commentators. One was given by Richard C. Bush, the former head of the American Institute in Taiwan (AIT). He focused on China's policy initiatives, including its "shift in Korean policy at the end of 2009, in favor of active measures to ensure that the North Korean state survived."[31] To him, the United States' Asia Pivot, announced in early January 2012, was actually caused by the "dynamics of China's revival as a great power," which, he noted, will be "much more complicated than previous periods of system transition." He even used instances of what he called "response by China's neighbors" as a corroboration of his point.[32] However, if we look at the individual cases

[30] Paul Denlinger, "Will China Do Something to Defend Their Position about the South China Sea Controversy?" Quora, retrieved, July 19, 2016, http://www.linkedin/pauldenlinger. Essentially, as he put it, "the aim of the Chinese government's policy is not to respond directly to Western and Western-media criticism on its South China Sea policy, . . .," because, he adds, it "is aware that some people, and the Western media especially, will criticize it no matter what it does, so why bother will what they say."

[31] Richard C. Bush, "The Response of China's Neighbors to the U.S. 'Pivot' to Asia," *Brookings: On Record*, January 31, 2012.

[32] Ibid.

of response he produced, the only unequivocal positive response in support of the United States' Asia Pivot came invariably from Japan and India. The other responses fell far short of substantiating his point. The Indonesian Foreign Minister, for example, expressed a commonly felt Asian concern for the "danger of vicious cycle of tensions and mistrust." The Prime Minister of Malaysia was worried about increased tensions (caused by the U.S. policy), while Singapore's Foreign Minister observed that ASEAN States wanted to avoid getting "caught between the competing interests" of the major powers, referring to both the United States and China.[33]

On the other hand, a contrary view on who or what started the action–reaction chain of events was given by Robert Kaplan, from the Center for a New American Security, a think tank in Washington, DC., and author of the celebrated book *Asian Cauldron* (2015). During the Q&A period at a Forum on "China's Reaction to the U.S. Pivot to Asia," sponsored by the Carnegie Endowment for International Peace, Kaplan said: "China is concerned because [the U.S. Asia Pivot] may mean the United States is trying to contain China. They see that the United States is sending 2,500 marines to Australia. Secretary of Defense Panetta said that under no circumstances will there be a smaller U.S. naval commitment in the Western Pacific. The Chinese are concerned that means the Americans are ganging up on them."[34]

The earlier two opposing views given by two competent analysts, on who or what initiated the chain of actions and reactions, represent not only a common perceptual division among bystander analysts. But the gap reflects also the division in the perceptions of the governments as well, as David Firestein has discovered in his study of the perception gap in the U.S.–China contest.[35]

---

[33] Ibid.

[34] Robert Kaplan, in a Q&A comment at the forum on "China's Response to the U.S. Pivot to Asia," Carnegie Endowment for International Peace, January 20, 2012.

[35] David J. Firestein, "The U.S.–China Perception Gap in the South China Sean," *The Diplomat*, August 19, 2016.

Firestein, Senior Vice President at the East-West Institute, notes that the United States and China look at the same set of facts, on SCS issues, through "very different perceptual lenses." He traces the bilateral perceptual gap to four different fundamental sources associated with their respective perceptual angles.

1. The first, and most fundamental, source for the perceptual gap, between the United States and China, revolves around "the actual definition and level of clarity of China's claims in the South China Sea." From the Chinese perspective, their claims in the SCS — broadly delineated by what China calls the Nine-Dash Line — "are highly grounded in history and clear-cut to the point of being self-evident and indisputable." But, in contrast, he adds, "the United States (along with other countries, claimants and non-claimants alike) perceives China's nine-dash-line claim — whatever its historical and legal merits — to be ill-defined and ambiguous."
2. The second, and related, reason for the perceptual gap is what Firestein calls the "history vs. law" divergence. By "law" here, he is referring to the U.S. view that UNCLOS III, alone, represents all there is to the international law of the sea and of territorial acquisition. "China," he notes, "takes the view that history is ultimately dispositive and that history trumps contemporary international law [UNCLOS III] in instances in which the two are in conflict." Firestein makes a reference to the "signing statements" that China made in 1996 (upon ratifying UNCOS III) and again in 2006, considering them to be "effectively 'grandfathering' [China's] own historical territorial and maritime claims where those views might be viewed by others as being incompatible with the terms of UNCLOS; and, respectively, rejecting key dispute resolution stipulations under UNCLOS." In an endnote (marked n. 3), Firestein remarks: "It should be noted, however, that China is not unique in issuing this kind of signing statement" (with a "grandfathering effect" in the legal sense). I wish to pause to make a brief comment. Throughout this book, our understanding of China's position on its SCS claim, broadly

delineated by the nine-dash-line — which encompasses the four major island groups and their adjacent waters — is that it is based on and protected by the "historic waters" principle in "general international law" (as opposed to treaty law, incl. UNCLOS III). It is, therefore, *general international law trumping treaty law*, not "history trumping law," as Firestein puts it. We have also noted, time and again, that the preamble of UNCLOS III stipulates "Matters that are not regulated by this Convention continue to be governed by the rule and principles of *general international law*." China, I wish to add, does not consider UNCLOS III relevant for the resolution of SCS disputes, such as in the Philippine–China arbitration case, for a reason different from what Firestein suggested in his "grandfathering" point. As spelled out in China's Position Paper filed with the PCA arbitral tribunal, China considers that matters concerning territorial sovereignty over maritime features in the SCS is "beyond the scope of the [UNCLOS III] Convention." Parenthetically, China lost the case to the Philippines, as we pointed out in Chapter 4, precisely because the Arbitral Tribunal did not look beyond UNCLOS III, which has nothing to say on "historic waters," to consider general international law, as it should have, per the admonition given in the preamble of UNCLOS III. That said, the "grandfathering" point made by Firestein, nevertheless, is a good lawyer's *obiter dictum* that further strengthens China's position.

3. The third reason that Firestein finds accountable for the U.S.–China perceptual gap is what he calls "the role of the Philippines and Vietnam." By that, he means the very different ways in which China and the United States, respectively, perceive of these two named Asian countries. China views both Vietnam and the Philippines as "instigators and trouble makers" in the SCS disputes. It "portrays both countries as the real aggressors — the countries that have been most active in altering and upsetting the status quo to their advantage, all while China has demonstrated great restraint in the face of their provocations." The United States, on the contrary, "views its ally (the Philippines)

and emerging partner (Vietnam) less as provocateurs and more as SCS claimants that have been bullied by a much larger and more powerful neighbor and claimant (China)." On the matter of land reclaiming (island building), Firestein continues, "the United States recognizes that both countries have reclaimed land in the South China Sea and even militarized islands, but it sees the scope of the Chinese efforts in these regards as far eclipsing, by orders of magnitude, that of the earlier Filipino and Vietnamese efforts. The United States sees China, not the Philippines and Vietnam, as the principal destabilizing force in the South China Sea in recent years." On its self-image, Firestein notes, "the United States regards itself as having been a force of restraint in the region, not an enabler, as the Chinese sometimes posit, of irresponsible and reckless actions on the part of the Philippines and Vietnam."

4. The fourth reason for the U.S.–China perceptual gap, according to Firestein, is simply that they follow their intuitive in their respective assessments of what happened. Beijing "believes that it is the United States, not China, that has upset the precarious balance (basically, the mostly "stable stalemate" that has obtained for some decades, up until recent years) with new, irrepressible, provocative, and destabilizing pronouncements and actions. As examples, the Chinese often point to the then-Secretary of State Hillary Clinton's 2010 statement that "the United States, like every nation, has a national interest in freedom of navigation, open access to Asia's maritime commons, and respect for international law in the South China Sea . . .and, more recently, U.S. freedom of navigation operations which have brought U.S. naval vessels into waters claimed by China as territorial (e.g., within 12 nautical miles of Chinese-claimed sovereign territory). Chinese interlocutors thus lay the responsibility for recent SCS-related bilateral tensions virtually entirely at the feet of the United States (as well as other players, such as the Philippines and Vietnam; more . . .)." In contrast, Firestein continues, "The United States has a diametrically opposed view. U.S. officials have stated that U.S. pronouncements and actions have been in direct response

to, and indeed proportionate to, Chinese policy departures and provocations and that the United States, not China, has been in [the] *reactive* mode" (emphasis added).

These last statements by Firestein, I hasten to acknowledge in agreement, seem to confirm what I said earlier about the tendency of each contending party to pass the blame to the other side, making a bystander analyst's job that much more difficult in trying to sort out the events, in order to determine who and what was responsible for that "action-1" which started all the chain of reactions, counterreactions, and counter to counterreactions, *ad infinitum*.

Tracing the Chain of Events: Forward and Backward in Time

Let us continue the same line of inquiry, and bring back the point about the sequence of events that unfolded. The U.S. side's standard version on the main reason why the U.S. navy was stepping up its patrolling and surveillance missions in the SCS is that it was "in response to" the Chinese construction of artificial islands in the SCS. On these artificial islands, so the U.S. pronouncement goes, the Chinese have even built runways and deployed military hardware, thus threatening the freedom of navigation on the high seas in violation of international law.[36]

If China should choose to respond, instead of just stonewalling all the Western finger pointing, its spokesman could have offered a very simple and powerful rebuttal conceived in two questions, including one from the standpoint of international law. The latter question can go like this: While China's island building in SCS is justifiable under international law (see below), can the United States pinpoint where under international law did it receive its authorization to play the role of an international "policeman" in the SCS by the use of its powerful navy?

[36] "Trump White House Vows to Stop China Taking South China Sea Islands," *Reuters News*, January 23, 2017.

Article 60 of the UNCLOS III provides for a coastal State's freedom to construct artificial islands. According to Art. 60(8), the difference in their legal status, when compared with natural islands, is that they (the artificial islands) "have no territorial sea of their own." Nothing under international law precludes the deployment of armaments on artificial islands. But, on the other hand, neither treaty law (including UNCLOS III) nor customary international law authorizes any particular State (not even the United States) to assume the role of a public "policeman" for the specific purpose of monitoring and enforcing the freedom of navigation.

The other question the imaginary Chinese spokesman could have raised is that the Chinese island building only began in 2014, but in contrast when was it that the U.S. navy began its patrolling of, and surveillance in, the SCS? The *New York Times* provided an answer when it reported an encounter, a near collision, in the SCS between American and Chinese naval vessels, in 2013.[37] The report said the U.S. carrier Cowpens was "observing the Chinese carrier, the Liaoning, as it made its first voyage in the South China Sea from its home base in Qingdao, the headquarters of China's North Sea Fleet." While the Chinese Defense Ministry did not respond to a *Times* request for comment on the maritime encounter, the U.S. side pinned the blame for the near collision on the Chinese side. No matter which side was truly responsible for the near collision, an outside observer might be tempted to draw an analogy of a similar (hypothetic) encounter, say, one that happened near the U.S. Navy base on the Kitsap Peninsula in the state of Washington, when a Chinese navy ship was observing the movement of a new American carrier.

When that (fictitious event) happens, one wonders what the U.S. side would say, especially if the Chinese side should parrot the usual American elocution that the Chinese ship was *patrolling* the Atlantic Ocean for the sake of protecting the freedom of navigation!

---

[37] "American and Chinese Navy Ships Nearly Collided in South China Sea," *New York Times*, December 14, 2013.

Returning to the same *New York Times* report earlier, the 2013 appearance of the Cowpens carrier in SCS, in fact, in the Chinese territorial waters, was not the first time that U.S. naval surveillance activity was found in China's backyard. The same *Times* report recalled an incident that happened back in 2009, in a near collision involving a surveillance ship, the Impeccable, with five Chinese ships in the SCS. With this background in mind, one can safely conclude that the start of the U.S. patrolling of the SCS was not occasioned by the Chinese island construction, which began only in 2014. The reverse is true, judging by the sequence of events when they took place.

Let us look backward in time to see what happened both in 2014 and the few years immediately before 2014, when the Chinese island building began. In a nutshell, we find that during 2014, the United Sates openly sided with Japan in the latter's smoldering disputes with China over the Diaoyu Island (the Japanese call it Senkaku). President Obama confirmed publicly during his visit in Tokyo that under Art. 5 of the U.S.–Japan alliance treaty, the United States will come to Japan's aid in the defense of the disputed island, if militarily threatened by China. Also in early 2014, the Vietnamese staged widespread and violent demonstrations against the Chinese over an oil drilling platform that was placed in a part of the SCS that even the Vietnamese Primer Minister Pham Van Dong had in 1958 recognized was under Chinese sovereignty. The United States, on that occasion, supported the Vietnamese instead, and rebuked the Chinese (as noted in Chapter 1). In 2013, the year immediately before, the Philippines, a U.S. ally, took the SCS dispute with China to arbitration before a PCA arbitral tribunal. In 2012, the year before that, the Obama Administration unveiled its Asia Pivot policy, which as we noted in Chapter 2, was a vaguely veiled attempt to line up Asian countries, including those in ASEAN and Japan, to contain China.

When one puts together all these events in their proper context and sequence, the only sensible conclusion that can be drawn is that the U.S.–China tensions in the SCS did not originate from Chinese provocation, to say the least, notwithstanding partisan quibbling to the contrary.

Chapter 7

The U.S.–China Contest (II): Risk of a Thucydides Trap (?)

I put a question mark after "Thucydides Trap" in the chapter's title to register my skepticism about the supposed similarity between the current China–U.S. face-off and the Athens–Sparta contest preceding the Peloponnesian War. There are, to me, at least three substantive reasons why the two situations are totally incompatible: (a) China is not a first-time upstart, but is on its second rise after a century and a half of decline, during which it learned that the world needed social justice and safeguards against the encroachments by the powerful against the weak, as discussed in Chapter 6. (b) The system of states in which China and the United States find themselves today, wrapped in a relationship that Richard Rosecrance depicts as "vulnerability interdependence,"[1] is qualitatively different from the ancient Greek

[1] "Vulnerability interdependence" means that the two economies are so intertwined that it's like there is a little bit of you in me, and a little bit of me in you, so that if one side wants to do anything to hurt the other, it is like committing suicide. Richard Rosecrance, "Power and International Relations: The Rise of China and its Effects,"

system of states where such interdependence was unknown between Athens and Sparta. (c) China's clout thus far is derived predominantly from its surging economic expansion; but its military might is not up to a level that would instill the sort of "fear" that the rising Athens did in Sparta, as Thucydides observed.

Thus, the China–U.S. clash of visions may not necessarily end in a Peloponnesian-type war, which would fulfill the parable of the Thucydides Trap, more especially if the distorted perceptions are duly corrected to jive with the facts-in-themselves. As we have noted in Chapter 6, President Trump reversed himself on his campaign pledge to declare China a currency manipulator, after he found out that the true reality contradicted his earlier gut feelings.

Nevertheless, for at least two reasons, many commentators are lured into believing that a war is inevitable from the on-going face-off between Washington and Beijing. One is the Neorealist international relations (IR) theory, backed by actual examples that unbalanced power, such as wielded by a rising emergent superpower (like the post-2010 China), is to be feared. This common apprehension is examined in Graham Allison's brand new book *Destined for War*, which drew on findings of the "Thucydides's Trap Case File," part of the Belfer Center's Applied History Project at Harvard University. The file has identified that 12 out 16 cases, over a period of 500 years, in which an ascending power challenged the prevailing dominant power, actually ended in war.[2] A common article of faith, in this school of thought, is that an overriding drive of a rising power is to attempt to *replace* the prevailing hegemonic power. Writings that expound this alarm abound in the literature. A ready example is *A Hundred Year Marathon: China's Secret Strategy to Replace America* (2015), by Michael Pillsbury, for four decades a veteran consultant to

International Studies Perspectives, vol. 7, no. 1 (2006): 31–35.

[2] Graham Allison, *Destined for War: Can America and China Escape Thucydides's Trap?* (Boston: Houghton Mifflin Harcort, 2017), p. 41ff. Allison, however, also noted that at least in four cases during the past 500 years the "rising and ruling powers successfully steered their ships of state through treacherous shoals without war," p. 187.

the Pentagon and U.S. intelligence agencies.[3] (As one cynical Chinese critic retorted, if it was indeed "China's *secret* strategy" as described, how would the author know it, unless he worked as a double agent!) The second reason for the belief that a U.S. war with the rising China is inevitable is supported by studies of the long tested U.S. foreign policy goal, which will not tolerate any other power establishing exclusive hegemonic control over Asia or the Pacific, ever since 1783.[4]

Knee-jerk reactions were found in Peter Navarro's *The Coming China War*,[5] and other provocative books that describe the U.S.–Chinese hassle in zero-sum terms. The notion of a "coming war on China" is so popular that it was co-opted to be the title of a documentary film. But, contrary to the impression the title may convey, the film, as its publicity blurb puts it, is "both a warning and an inspiring story of people's resistance to war and . . . challenges the notion and propaganda of China as a new enemy."[6]

Speculations on a violent outcome approached an increasing crescendo in the wake of the Donald Trump election campaign in 2016, which one writer characterized as a cacophony of "impressiveness, combativeness, and impulsiveness." Yet, so much of it has "survived the transition into the presidency" as to prompt the same writer to express his concerns about "a vision of Trump at war." His article was published in the *Foreign Affairs* (May–June, 2017), in a special issue under the rubric of "Present at the Destruction: Trump in Practice."[7] Separated by a few pages later in the same issue, another commentator toiled to lament Asia's transition "from pivot to peril" in the "Trump era."[8]

---

[3] Michael Pillsbury, *The Hundred Year Marathon* (New York: Henry Holt, 2015).

[4] Michael J. Green, *By More than Providence: Grand Strategy and American Power in the Asia Pacific Since 1783* (New York: Columbia University Press, 2017).

[5] Peter Navarro, *The Coming China Wars* (Upper Saddle River: FT Press, 2006).

[6] The Coming War on China, a film directed by John Pilger, disseminated by Bullfog Films, in Oley, Pa 19547.

[7] Philip Gordon, "A Vision of Trump at War: How the President Could Stumble into Conflict," *Foreign Affairs*, vol. 96, no. 3 (2017), 10–19.

[8] Bilahari Kausikan, "Asia in the Trump Era: From Pivot to Peril?" *Foreign Affairs*, vol. 96, no. 3 (2017), 146–53.

To sum up, most of these articulated worries about a violent ending to the U.S.–China contest, following China's unstoppable rise, were probably indicative of honest human aspirations for peace and orderliness in world affairs, on the part of concerned citizens. If there is anything in common among them, it is their intuitive assumption that interactions between the prevailing dominant power (the United States) and a rising (rerising) power (China) are in the nature of a zero-sum game. This assumption seems to be supported, at the epistemological level, by the Western culture since Socrates that casts serious doubt on the reconciliation of opposites. If this is true, then, there is a ray of hope away from the trap of the war frenzy, as much as the Chinese, at least their leadership, are not similarly guided by a culture-induced faith that the clash of opposites is inevitable. Time and again, President Xi Jinping has unequivocally, and emphatically, stressed that "the Pacific Ocean is vast enough to accommodate ... two great powers in the world."[9] The Confucian-Daoist culture taught the Chinese not only that opposites can be reconciled but also that, if managed well, they may be made to work in synergy. True to this tradition, the Chinese since Deng Xiaoping have been able to unite socialism and market economy, two distinctively diametrical opposites, in such a way that the result shows "one plus one is larger than two."[10] Hence, their "socialist-market economy with Chinese characteristics" was able to see the nation's gross domestic product (GDP) increased 20 times in three decades, making China the world's second largest economy by 2014, next only to the United States.

It takes two to tango, but, it is obvious, if one side does not join in, there will be no tango. The good thing is that the Chinese do not share the Western (U.S.) belief that the ascent of a rising (rerising)

[9] The first time he pounced on this theme was in his first meeting with President Obama, at the Annenberg Estate, during his 2012 state visit to America. He repeated the same theme during Obama's return state visit in Beijing in 2014. The following year, Xi reiterated the idea to John Kerry, the U.S. Secretary of State, when he was visiting China, in 2015.

[10] On how the two opposites (socialism and market economy) have been made to work in synergism, see James C. Hsiung, *China into its Second Rise*, Chaps. 6 and 7 (Singapore: World Scientific, 2012).

power will be doomed to an inevitable conflict with the existing hegemonic power, at least not on the same ground — that is, militarily. This can be seen from China's deliberately chosen strategy, pursuing a geo-economic course (see below), aimed at choreographing a "nonsymmetric" competition with the United States, which is still, mentally, mired in the geopolitical game of the Cold War era.

Differing U.S. and Chinese Strategies for Competition

Despite all the earlier speculations about an armed conflict to erupt from the United States–China square-off, what will determine the final outcome, I think, rests with whether the strategies that the two countries opted to pursue put them on a straight military collision course. For its part, the United States' set strategy can be summed up as one conceived mainly in militarization, or, more specifically, naval militarization in the Asia Pacific, in particular, in the South China Sea. This strategy, known in the Pentagon as The Asia-Pacific Maritime Security Strategy, is codified as the Carl Levin and Howard P. "Buck" McKeon National Defense Authorization Act.[11]

A spin-off from this strategy, for instance, was the dispatch of a U.S. warship, the U.S.S. Dewey, to within 12 nautical miles of a Chinese-owned islet, known as Mischief Reef in English (or Yongshu Jiao, 永暑礁 in Chinese), in the Spratly island group. The U.S. patrol, the first of its kind since October, 2016, was described in the media as "the latest attempt to counter what Washington sees as China's attempts to limit freedom of navigation in the strategic waters" of the South China Sea.[12]

On the other hand, and fortunately, the Chinese chose not to compete with the United States in the military domain. Their strategy, pursued under the leadership of President Xi Jinping, focused more on variable-sum geo-economics, rather than zero-sum

[11] Public Law 113–291.

[12] "South China Sea: U.S. Warship Challenges China's Claims with First Operation under Trump," *CNN News*, May 25, 2017, and "U.S. Warship Challenges China's Claims in South China Sea," *Aljazeera News*, May 25, 2017, p. 201.

geopolitics. Since late 2012, when Xi was elected the General Secretary of the Chinese Communist Party, anticipating his confirmation by the National People's Congress (NPC, the legislature) as the President of the PRC in early 2013, he has masterminded and brokered the launch of three geo-economic initiatives: (a) the New Development Bank (NDB), under the BRICS grouping (comprising Brazil, Russia, India, China, and South Africa); (b) the Asian Infrastructure Investment Bank (AIIB); and (c) the One Belt and One Road (OBOR) project. Xi's ultimate purpose in orchestrating these three geo-economic initiatives, which is not fully understood by Washington, is to stage a "nonsymmetric competition" (a term I coined) with the United States. Simply put, it is to steer the U.S.–China competition away from the military orbit into a geo-economic one, capitalizing on China's economic dynamism, and skirting a military rivalry that may court consequences that will benefit neither side.

A brief introduction is in order to this peculiar Chinese geo-economic strategy. Of the three named initiatives, the first one launched is the NDB, under the joint sponsorship of the BRICS, which began operational in 2016, with its headquarters in Shanghai, headed by an Indian, K. V. Kamath, as its first elected president. It is sometimes described as an "IMF clone" institution, with an initial capitalization of US$100 billion. Its stated purpose is to mobilize resources in support of infrastructure and sustainable development projects within the BRICS and in other emerging economies, complementing the existing efforts of multilateral and regional development banks. Unlike in the Bretton Woods institutions (i.e., IMF and World Bank), the NDP does not have a weighted voting system; and decision-making is based on an equal-share principle, despite the fact that China's GDP is bigger than the other four members combined. During its first year in operation, the Bank doled out $811 million, out of a total $1.5 billion loan commitment, for the funding of green energy projects in four BRICS member nations: Brazil ($300 mn), India ($250 mn), South Africa ($180 mn), and China ($81 mn).[13]

[13] "BRICS Bank Announces First Set of Loans," *The BRICS Post*, April 16, 2016.

The next geo-economic initiative, the AIIB, was a Chinese brainchild, following a 2010 survey by the regional Asian Development Bank (ADB) that found Asia's need for infrastructure investment to top $8 trillion for the next decade. The same report also noted "impediments" in financing this gigantic need.[14] The AIIB was therefore an answer to the challenge posed by this gap between the funding needs and the financing impediments identified by the ADB. Launched in Beijing in 2014, it began operational in 2015. The United Nations addressed its launch as having the potential for "scaling up financing for sustainable development" for the concern of global economic governance. The initial capital of the bank is $100 billion, equivalent to two-thirds of the capital of the ADB and about half that of the World Bank.

The AIIB started with 57 founding member states, including 37 from the Asian region, and 20 from other regions. Some in the latter group came from Europe, including Britain, a staunch U.S. ally, whose application to join the AIIB was unsuccessfully opposed by Washington. Three more of America's European allies, Germany, France, and Italy, followed the example of, first, Luxemburg, and, then, Britain in joining the AIIB. Among the initial regional members were India and seven members of the Association of Southeast Asian Nations (ASEAN) that included the Philippines, a U.S. ally in Asia. Although U.S. pressures allegedly kept Singapore and Australia from signing up as the founding members, Singapore joined after the October 24, 2014, signing ceremony in Beijing. And, Australia joined one year later.[15] In March 2017, AIIB approved the joining of 13 additional member states, enlarging its total membership to a hefty 70.

If financing, logistical, and governance issues are addressed successfully, AIIB could be lending $20 billion a year in 2020, not far off the $29.7 billion annual loan commitments of the World Bank in FY2016.

All this, however, is a complementary sideshow to the OBOR project, designed initially to bind together 65 countries at the time it

[14] ADB Working Paper Series, No. 229 (July 2010).

[15] By Shannon Tiezzi, "China's AIIB: The Final Tally," *The Diplomat*, April 17, 2015.

was launched in 2014, but the number of the countries attracted to it, according to one source, swelled to 77 in 2015, and 110 in 2017.[16]

The name of OBOR, which is sometimes also acronymed BRI, derived from "Belt and Road Initiative," recalls the historical Silk Road linking China with Asia Minor and parts of Europe. It now consists of an on-land Economic Belt and a Maritime Silk Road. Together, the on-land and maritime wings of the project will link up, in one gigantic infrastructure and trade network, more than 65, possibly up to 110, different economies in Asia, Middle East, Europe, and Africa. The $1 trillion funding will come from a number of sources, including China's Silk Road Fund and the multilateral AIIB. One source gave China's investment as having surpassed $50 billion, plus the additional $14.5 billion that President Xi pledged at the May 15, 2017 Belt and Road Forum in Beijing that would funnel into the Silk Road Fund.[17]

The land-bound Belt will start from Xi'an (西安) in Western China, across Pakistan and the five Central Asia republics, before entering Iran, Russia, Turkey, and onto Europe. It will involve creation of highways, railways, pipelines, aviation facilities, telecommunications, and power networks.

The maritime "Road" is designed to link the South China Sea with the Indian Ocean, East Africa, the Red Sea, and the Mediterranean. It drew its inspiration from the voyages made during the Ming Dynasty, under the command of the eunuch Admiral Zheng He (Cheng Ho), in the 15th century.

The long-term economic and political goals of OBOR are threefold: (a) to embrace a form of open governance in the management of the global infrastructure and trade network, (b) to create a centripetal momentum toward China from all regions, and (c) to develop the Chinese Renminbi (RMB) as a reserve currency of member nations.[18]

---

[16] Hugh White, "China's Belt and Road Initiative to Challenge U.S.-led Order," *East Asian Forum*, May 8, 2017.

[17] Shannon Tiezzi, "What Did China Accomplish at the Belt and Road Forum," *The Diplomat*, May 16, 2017.

[18] James J. Griffiths, "Just What Is This One Belt, One Road Thing Anyway?" *CNN.com*, May 11, 2017; Also Tian Jinchen, "One Belt and One Road Connecting China and the World," *McKinsey Co.*, July 2016.

According to one report,[19] this initiative is expected to create jobs and opportunities for people and businesses along the routes as well as companies and investors around the world in areas such as infrastructure, finance, trading, logistics, and professional services. Opening up trade corridors will also make it easier for businesses going into and out of China to reach the growing middle classes, which could number more than 4 billion by 2021. In the decade that follows, it is anticipated that 66% of the world's middle class will live in Asia — many along the Belt and Road. As a result, there will be an increasing demand for a wide range of goods and services as more people become major consumers with a growing disposable income for the first time. According to Stuart Gulliver, Group Chief Executive for HSBC Holdings, "The American dream of the 20th century is becoming the Asian dream of the 21st. A house, a car, a smartphone, travel, banking services, healthcare — the prospect of unfettered upward social mobility for many more families."[20]

The OBOR initiative will begin by building or improving the physical infrastructure along these routes including rail lines, ports, power grids, and telecommunications networks — which will facilitate the flow of these goods and services. Infrastructure projects will be funded by strengthening the existing financial framework of lending and capital raising, and will be further supported through new or enhanced customs, taxation, and trade and investment policy conditions aimed at making trade between countries easier and stimulating economic growth.

RMB Internationalization

China has already overtaken Japan to become the world's second largest provider of overseas direct investment, partly as the result of the BRI; and infrastructure remains the dominant theme along the route. Even when Beijing policymakers raised interest rates in 2017 in reaction to the strong U.S. dollar, they continued to open channels of capital outflows. For example, the Shenzhen/Hong Kong Stock

---

[19] HSBC, "Reshaping the Future World Economy," May 15, 2017.

[20] Ibid.

Connect was launched in December 2016 and there were plans to start a bond connect program in a few months. There are signs that Beijing remains committed to capital account liberalization. It is clear that China is continuing its steady integration with the global economy through a new phase of overseas investment and RMB internationalization, particularly as the BRI (or OBOR) picks up momentum. In the long term, according to the HSBC, a global banking institution, China is expected to be a leader in the next phase of globalization that will help drive economic growth around the world.[21]

If these trends continue, it means that China's strategy in pursuing a nonsymmetric competition with the United States has proven to serve its interests impressively. And, there is no reason why China should abandon the successful strategy focusing on geo-economics, and staying away from competing with the United States in a "zero-sum" geopolitical game. Be that as it may, one commentator, speaking for many others, raised the unavoidable question: Who, between the United States and China, will be the top superpower in 50 years? And, his answer is:

> China will probably have a large economy in 50 years, but the US GDP per capita will still be much larger. On top of that, the US has an unchallenged military logistics network. With more aircraft carriers than the rest of the world combined, top-of-the-line technology, and a global span and size to match, the US has a presence and/or impact in nearly every area of the globe … The US both created and defined what a superpower does, and the standard can get pretty expensive. China lacks the soft power, military logistics, and span to match US impact now, and I'm not sure that will change that drastically.[22]

In other words, the success of China's chosen geo-economic strategy is judged by whether its ultimate purpose is achieved in keeping its competition with the United States as an "unsymmetric" one,

[21] HSBC, "Silk Road globalizes the renminbi," May 15, 2017.

[22] H. L. Cowan, "Who Will Be the Top Superpower 50 Years from Now?" *The Local American Neocon*, June 23, 2017.

staying away from military competition. This translates into a lack of intention, on China's part, to try to "replace" the United States as the top superpower, notwithstanding Michael Pillsbury's allegation to the contrary.[23]

Barring unforeseen turns and twists, a nonviolent ending to the current U.S.–China contest seems to be within the realm of the possible. In other words, a war is not in the cards, despite all the prophecies of doom.

Conclusion

In his well-documented book, Graham Allison noted that in the past 500 years, the data showed at least four cases in which "rising and ruling powers successfully steered their ships of state through treacherous shoals without war." These were exceptions to the pattern established in the same 500 years in which 12 out of the 16 cases resulted in war between rising and ruling powers, confirming the parable of the Thucydides Trap.

The first on the list of the four exceptions was when Spain rose to replace Portugal in the late 15th and early 16th centuries. The rise of Germany to dominate Europe since the end of the Cold War is the second, and most recent, such case of exception. And, the next two cases came during the 20th century: The United States deposed the United Kingdom as the leading global power; and the Soviet Union threatened America's position as the unipolar power.[24] Just as he hoped at the end of his book, it looks from our discussions above that the rise of China is "destined" to be the fifth exception. There is not going to be a repeat of the Thucydides Trap, and the question mark I placed after the term in the title of this chapter above is more than warranted.

---

[23] See Note 3.

[24] Graham Allison, *Destined for War*, p. 187ff.

Chapter

8

The Way Out of the Legal and Geopolitical Tangles: From the "China Threat" Scare to a New World Order

This book is about the threats to peace due to the long, drawn-out disputes over the South China Sea (SCS) between the competing claimants, but culminating in a gratuitous crisis over the U.S.–China contest, sustained by Washington's geopolitical instincts. Although it advances no claim to any part of SCS, the United States is alarmed by the rise of China, and the attendant "China threat" scare trumpeted by many International Relation (IR) neorealists and media gurus alike.

As we have seen in Chapter 6, among other things, Washington's perception that Vietnam and the Philippines, among the SCS claimants, were "bullied by a much larger and more powerful neighbor and claimant China" further captured U.S. vigilance toward the SCS disputes.[1] As a nonclaimant, the only legitimate pretext for the U.S. naval excursions into the SCS was that China's island building in the maritime region presented a threat to international freedom of navigation (FON). As we have also seen, the FON pretext has served as a convenient alibi to obfuscate the truth of the U.S. reflex to the "China threat" scare. The SCS, thus, provides a stage on which the drama of the U.S. attempt to stem China's expanding influence has been unfolding.

In our search for a way out of the legal and geopolitical tangles surrounding the doomsday SCS tensions, our task begins with tackling of the myth of the "China threat" scare. For its part, the least that China can do is to seek exoneration from the stigma of a scofflaw that came with its repudiation of the award handed down in 2016 by the Permanent Court of Arbitration (PCA) tribunal in the Philippines–China arbitration, as discussed in Chapter 4. A full exoneration from this legal stigma could only come from adjudicative means; there is no other way.

In the ensuing paragraphs, we will first address the question of how best to assess China's rise, by examining the varied assessments by governments and commentators, which seemed to have undergone noticeable changes over time. Next, we will entertain the ticklish question of how China might best exonerate itself by resorting to an adjudicative recourse, rather than sticking to its repudiation of the PCA arbitral award, or just quietly licking its wound, as it were, in sultry defiance.

Interpreting China's Rerise: Dissidence and Shifts in the Intellectual Climate[2]

To be true, different governments have varied shades of opinion on China's rise, based on their respective perceptions. By the same token,

[1] David Firestein, "The U.S.-China Perception Gap in the South China Sea." *The Diplomat*, August 19, 2016. Note 35, Chapter 6 above.

[2] In this section, I am relying on my discussions in "The Changing Intellectual and Political Climate in the China Debate and the Future of IR Theory," *American Foreign Policy Issues*, vol. 30, no. 1 (February 2008): 1–12, published by the National Committee on American Foreign Policy (NCAFP); and Hsiung, *China into Its Second Rise* (Singapore: World Scientific, 2012), pp. 221–32; "Utility and Inadequacy of Realist Theory: Assessing China's Rise," *International Studies Review*, vol. 17, no. 1 (March 2015), 132ff.

there is a separate body of idiosyncratic perceptions among political analysts that are at variance with one another, on the question of the alleged China threat. Again, just as perceptions may shift with deeper observations over time, which may bring the perceived reality closer in line with the true reality (the facts-in-themselves), the China threat theory has undergone several waves of change that deserve our attention as to its relevance to U.S.–China policy.

At the turn of the new century, when the robust Chinese economy proved to be the only one that had successfully withstood the world's worst financial crisis in the late 1990s,[3] continuing its brisk growth rate of 9%–11% annually. China became the envy, and fear, of the West. More scary were forecasts by respectable pundits that China was poised to catch up with the United States economically by 2025 and militarily by mid-century.[4] Hence, the hue and cry of the "China Threat" took off relentlessly.

Following the same cue, scholarly warnings about an emerging Chinese hegemony swarmed the published literature, to an extent unmatched since the erstwhile warnings about the Soviet threat on the eve of the Cold War. The best known, and most blunt, example was probably the *mega opus* by John Mearsheimer at the University of Chicago. Writing in the *Foreign Affairs* in 2001,[5] Mearsheimer called for a reversal of America's engagement policy, and suggested that U.S. interests would be best served by keeping China down and encouraging Japan to build up its military capability, to help cope with the China threat.

If Mearsheimer was speaking for the mainstream realist IR scholars at the time, there have since been unforeseen shifts in the intellectual climate surrounding the China debate. To begin with, there has been a discernible shift away from the realist paradigm, a shift that

---

[3] The first post-Cold War financial crisis broke out in northern Europe in the early 1990s. The second hit Latin America in 1994–1995; and the third, and most severe, financial crisis hit the "Tigers" in East Asia, during 1997–1999. But, China escaped the last one unscathed, because of its macroeconomic control.

[4] A typical version of these predictions was found in Ronald L. Tammen, et al., *Power Transitions: Strategies for the 21st Century* (New York: Seven Bridges Press, 2000).

[5] John F. Mearsheimer, "The Future of the American Pacifier," *Foreign Affairs*, vol. 80, no. 5 (September–October 2001): 46–61, 47.

can in part be traced to the fact that Chinese behavior has had a showing that did not follow the paths predicted by most realists. Earlier, for example, Kenneth Waltz, arguably the best-known spokesman for the realist school since Hans Morgenthau, had predicted that secondary states such as China, Japan, and Russia would seek to balance U.S. power in the post-Cold War era.[6] His view was shared by Christopher Layne, among other realists.[7] And, it certainly reinforced Mearsheimer's thinking that a rising China would seek dominance at the expense of the United States, the world's prevailing hegemon.[8]

However, from observing that China has not tried to balance the United States but instead has been bandwagoning to it, Peter Van Ness (at Australian National University), for one, speculates that the stiff hierarchy in the present system may provide an answer why the realist view is not borne out empirically.[9] Quite to the contrary, as Steve Chan points out, it is the United States that is trying to balance against China, which does not even possess 80% of the U.S. military power — a threshold held by the power transition theory to be necessary if a rising power (like China) is going to challenge the extant hegemon (the United States).[10]

Following in the same vein, David Kang (then at Dartmouth College) also raises a question as to why Thailand and other Asian secondary states in the region are not balancing China in "the same way that the United States balanced the Soviet Union."[11] Extrapolating

---

[6] Kenneth N. Waltz, "Structural Realism after the Cold War," *International Security*, vol. 23, no. 1 (summer, 2000): 32, 41.

[7] Cf., for example, Christopher Layne, "The Unipolar Illusion: Why New Great Powers Will Arise," *International Security*, vol. 17, no. 3 (Spring 1993): 5–51.

[8] This fear is echoed in Martin Jacques, *When China Rules the World: The End of the West and the Birth of a New Global Order* (New York: The Penguin Press, 2009).

[9] Peter Van Ness, "Hegemony, Not Anarchy: Why China and Japan Are Not Balancing U.S. Unipolar Power," *International Relations of the Asia-Pacific*, vol. 2, no. 2 (2002): 131–50.

[10] Steve Chan, *Looking for Balance: China, the United States, and Power Balancing in East Asia* (Palo Alto: Stanford University Press, 2012), p. 223f.

[11] David Kang, "Hierarchy, Balancing, and Empirical Puzzles in Asian International Relations," *International Security*, vol. 28, no. 3 (Winter 2003–2004): 165–89, 172.

from his previous studies of over five centuries of East Asian IRs, Kang finds that bandwagoning to, not balancing against, the hegemon is the typical behavior of secondary states in a system of steep hierarchy, such as in the Asian Tribute System of yore.[12]

The return, coincidental or not, of mainstream scholarly interest in *hierarchy* — which David Lake (UC-San Diego) calls "one of the dead horses" in the IR literature[13] — represents a major wave of intellectual climate change in the literature on the rise of China. It calls into question the adequacy of the realist paradigm. This slight shift from realist "anarchy" (i.e., lack of a supranational authority over states) to "hierarchy" (a structure dominated by a hegemon that calls the shots), and from power balancing to bandwagoning by secondary states, opened the floodgates to a widening debate on whether the earlier realist fixation with power and power balancing can adequately explain, or anticipate, the behavior of a rising power such as China.

Picking up on the theme of hierarchy as a structure of IRs, Lake develops a derivative point regarding the importance of (moral) authority in the conduct of hegemonic foreign policy, if the United States is going to lead. Appling this framework to the future East–West relations, he sees that conflict with rising powers, especially China, is not "foreordained." Rather, it is in part a function of the policy choices of the United States, the existing hegemon. By building authority, rather than relying purely on brute power, he explains, the United States will have enough followings in the world, when it has to face a future Chinese superpower. The United States, he adds, "might even succeed in locking China into an American-dominated international order."[14]

Rethinking IR theory may take other forms, too, but all was tweaked by a curiosity about the prospect of a rising China. For

---

[12] Kang can find support from Eric Labs, "Do Week States Bandwagon?" *Security Studies*, vol. 1, no. 3 (Spring 1992): 41–61.

[13] David Lake, "The New Sovereignty in International Relations," *International Studies Review*, vol. 4, no. 5 (2003): 303–23.

[14] Ibid., 303. Indicative of the return of scholarly interest in hierarchy is Katja Weber's, *Hierarchy Amist Anarchy* (Albany: State University Press, 2000).

example, Jacek Kugler, at the Claremont Graduate University, who collaborated with the late Alfred Organski in developing the "power transition" theory, stepped forward to fine-tune, or clarify, the theory itself. According to the original "power transition" theory, as is generally understood by most IR students, war is most likely when power is roughly equal. Kugler is now emphasizing what has been said in fine print, but often overlooked, in the power transition theory, as it was first formulated on the basis of historical examples, namely: that "such a war is likely *only* when the parties fundamentally disagree about the status quo."[15] Thus, an advice offered by Kugler is that the United States should focus on Asia far more than on the Global War on Terror. "The path to international peace," he stressed, "can be ensured if action is taken to enhance satisfaction by China and other growing giants in Asia" (Id., p. 36). This counsel coincided with the Bush Administration's reordering of its priorities by naming China a "stakeholder" in the global system, about the same time.

Another challenge to the realist reflex on the China threat, representing still another shift in the intellectual climate, is from Richard Rosecrance, an international political economy (IPE) expert at Harvard, who weighs in by calling attention to the transformation of the Westphalian system as a result of the post-Cold War economic globalization. Realist theory, which is too closely tied to the preglobalization past, with its geopolitical preoccupation, can no longer adequately explain the behavior of states in the new IRs, he laments. Before going on to offer his main points about the changed international system today, he first examines the different implications of power. Noting that power is a protean attribute, he points out that "the amount of power that a nation possesses does not dictate its policy or behavior." What matters is *intention*. There is no inevitability of war occurring as a result of one power overtaking an extant hegemonic state. The result depends on whether the newly powerful state has expansive intentions. At the turn of the

[15] Jacek Kugler, "The Asian Ascent: Opportunity for Peace or Precondition for War?" *International Studies Perpectives*, vol. 7, no. 1 (2006): 36–42, 39.

20th century, he notes, the United States overtook Great Britain without war. In economic terms, Japan moved ahead of the Soviet Union in 1983, but neither country was tempted to fight over the transition.[16] I might add that in the opening decades of the 20th century, both Germany and France were locked in a fierce arms race. But, France remained defensive all along. Only Germany turned expansive. What accounted for the difference was their disparate intentions.

In addition to asking if China has the intention to challenge U.S. hegemonic power, Rosecrance counsels, one has to note the different world system in which China finds itself today. Because of economic globalization, China will enter a world market in which "many of the spoils have already been appropriated" (Id., p. 34). In the world of 1914, he adds, great powers (i.e., Britain, France, Germany, etc.) were not dependent upon the commercial ties forged among them. Those ties could be replaced by other suppliers and markets. Foreign direct investments (FDI) did not flow between the major powers, but from the metropolis to the colonies, even then in small amounts.

In the world of the 21st century, however, Chinese industries, although growing rapidly, may often be subsidiaries (or joint-venture partners) of major world corporations located elsewhere. In the age of what Rosecrance calls "vulnerability interdependence," not even the United States can boast of having attained unipolarity of economics, despite its overwhelming military might. For the Chinese, it means their country will be studded with foreign firms — including United States, Japanese, European firms — contributing the needed technology for its development (Id., p. 34). Hence, it is unlikely that China will be so insane as to seek self-destruction by trying to destroy the existing system. Economic ties and cooperation with foreign powers, including the United States, Japan, Russia, European Union, India, and so on, will be preferable to military expansion against them, so concludes Rosecrance.

---

[16] Richard Rosecrance, "Power and International Relations: The Rise of China and Its Effects," *International Studies Perspectives*, vol. 7, no. 1: 31–35, 32.

Signaling still another change in the intellectual climate, there is a slight *geographic* shift as well. Instead of the earlier "Pacific Century,"[17] there began talks about an "Asian Century." As Abramowitz and Bosworth put it, "much more than a geographic expression, East Asia is now an international economic power." What led them to this conclusion is, essentially, a few statistics. For example, East Asia's share of global gross domestic product (GDP) has risen sharply from some 12% in 1970 to nearly 20% in 2004. Its share of global trade has grown even more rapidly, from 10% in 1975 to 21% in 2003. The world's nonagricultural labor force has doubled in only a decade as East Asian workers have entered the global economy. And, alarmingly, East Asian central banks now hold some $2 trillion in American assets.[18] If Japan used to be thought of as constituting the powerful moving force in East Asia, it has phased out from Asia's center stage, following its decade and a half long economic morass. Since the turn of the new century, increasingly some commentators are beginning to lump China and India together, known as "Chindia," [19] as a force that will excel at the high end and the low end, and in services as well as in manufacturing. A report by the Economist Intelligence Unit, released on March 30, 2006, even forecasts that by 2020 the combined GDP of India and China will be 39% of the global GDP, and that Asia's total GDP will double that of the United States.[20] Some quarters are hedging their bets and began to promote India as an Asian competitor of China. The *Far Eastern Economic Review* (March

---

[17] The term "Pacific Century" was heralded by Staffan B. Linder, *The Pacific Century: Economic and Political Consequences of Asian-Pacific Dynamism* (Stanford: Stanford University Press, 1986); William McCord, *The Dawn of the Pacific Century* (New Brunswick: Transaction Publishers, 1991); Mark Borthwick, *Pacific Century* (Boulder: Westview Press, 1992), among others.

[18] Morton Ambramowitz and Stephen Bosworth, "America Confronts the Asian Century," *Current History*, vol. 105, no. 690 (April 2006): 147–52, 147. The article was based on their forthcoming book (Century Foundation Press, 2006).

[19] Clyde Prestowitz, "'Chindia' Tilts the Playing Field," *Current History*, vol. 105, no. 690 (April 2006):148–49.

[20] The report was carried in *Qiao Bao* (New York: the China Press), March 31, 2006, p. A2.

2006: 12–17), for example, featured an article titled: “India’s Coming Eclipse of China.” The *Economist* (June 3, 2006, p. 13) even reports that “India is producing more world-class companies than China. The best known are wizards of software and ‘business process outsourcing’ — Indian firms have two-thirds of the global market in offshore IT services and half that in BPO,” a reference to job outsourcing.

While the media is celebrating the “Rise of India” and its potential teaming up with America,[21] the fact is that Europe is already “in a funk” about an “Indian invasion” (*Economist*, June 3, 2006, p. 13). In the United States, especially in Congress, the news that India is a stronger (than China) market of business process outsourcing (BPO) from advanced economies seems to have taken some edge off China’s alleged sin of drawing away America’s jobs because of outsourcing.

When the focus is turned away from China to the “Asian century,” more and more analysts are directing their attention to why China’s Asian neighbors, with the obvious exception of Taiwan, are not as worried about the China threat as American officials think they should be. Abramowitz and Bosworth, for example, were even more specific than David Kang,[22] who was the first one to raise that same question. They noted that Secretary of Defense Donald Rumsfeld, while attending a 2005 security conference in Singapore, asked a hawkish question, namely: Since no nation threatens China, why is China increasing its investment in the building of new weapons systems? Abramowitz and Bosworth turned the question around and asked Rumsfeld: As no nation threatens the United States, why is America’s total defense expenditure bigger than the total defense expenditures of all the rest of the world combined?

The coauthors question the validity of the Pentagon’s mind-set, as represented by Rumsfeld’s question, which they term “ludicrous.” If one follows the Pentagon’s mind-set, then one would have assumed

---

[21] See the special issue highlighting The Rise of India, *Foreign Affairs*, vol. 85, no. 4 (July/August 2006): 2–57; Fareed Zakaria, “India Rising,” in *Newsweek*, March 6, 2006, pp. 31–42.

[22] David Kang, “Getting Asia Wrong: The Need for New Analytical frameworks,” *International Security*, vol. 27, no. 4 (Spring 2003): 57–85.

that China's escalating power would cause countries in the Asian region to value America's presence more highly. But, Abramowitz and Bosworth hasten to point out that, in reality, only Japan, among China's neighbors, has moved to enhance its alliance with the United States (p. 150). I might add that the reason for Japan to do so is due to a running saga of animosity deeply rooted in history, which is only exacerbated by Tokyo's intense feud with China over the vast East China Sea oil and gas resources.[23]

As an update, it may be noted that Rumsfeld's successor in the Pentagon, Robert Gates, did not share his paranoid view of China. Speaking before the same forum in Singapore, the Shangri-La Dialogue, on June 2, 2007, Secretary Gates expressed optimism about U.S. relations with China, and downplayed a Pentagon report released only days before he left Washington, regarding Beijing's stepped-up military buildup. In contrast to Rumsfeld's harsh language assailing the Chinese threat two years before, Gates only expressed concern about the opaqueness of China's defense spendings. He quickly switched his discussion to more recent increased military-to-military contacts at all levels between the United States and China. During a recent visit to China, he noted, General Peter Pace, Chairman of the Joint Chiefs of Staff, even sat in the cockpit of the top-of-the-line Chinese fighter.[24] Earlier in Washington, on March 8, 2007, Secretary Gates shared space at a media roundtable with General Pace, about China. While Gates cautioned that the higher Chinese defense spendings "did not reveal much about China's intentions," General Pace stated that it was expected that, like the United States, China would attempt to move ahead should it find a "gap" in its military capabilities.[25]

---

[23] See my "Sea Power, the Law of the Sea, and the Sino-Japanese East China Sea "Resource War," *American Foreign Policy Interests*, vol. 27, no. 6 (December 2005): 513–30.

[24] See an AFP report, "Gates Optimistic about China Despite Military Buildup," retrieved http://www.iiss.org/whats-news/iiss-in-the-press/june-2007/gates-optimistic-about-china-despite buildup.

[25] As reported by AFP/Reuters, March 8, 2007, online.

The most telling of the change in the intellectual climate, concerning the China debate, is in the subtle but real shift in John Mearsheimer's own position. Six years after his 2000 article in the *Foreign Affairs*, Mearsheimer wrote an update article in the April 2006 issue of *Current History*. Under the ticklish title of "China's Unpeaceful Rise,"[26] he continued to reason as a realist, flaunting his "theory of international politics that says the mightiest states will attempt to establish hegemony in their region of the world while making sure no rival great power dominates another region" (p. 160). However, unlike other realists before (including himself), he introduced an extraneous variable, which is "intentions," next to the habitual realist analytical tools of anarchy and power (capability). This "intention" variable recalls a similar point made by Richard Rosecrance above. Although Mearsheimer attempts to appear consistent between his two articles, separated by six years in between, his introduction of "intention," a volitional-subjective element, side by side with the two nonvolitional attributes of the realist "system" (i.e., anarchy and power), transforms the basic assumption in realist thinking that the system's attributes — principally the power distribution across the system — dictate states' behavior. To realists, all behavior of states is system induced. The introduction of a volitional-subjective factor (intention), reflecting a possible influence of constructivism, changes one's whole outlook on whether and how China is to be a threat. If China does not demonstrate an intention to challenge the existing world order, or if other states (including the ruling hegemon) do not find (perceive) an intention on the part of the rising Chinese superpower to seek to dominate others, then there is not necessarily going to be a hegemonic war. This is so, because war, in this theoretical outlook, is no longer automatic, or induced by the system's power distribution. A logical derivation, therefore, is that whether the rising China is going to be a threat does not purely depend on China alone. Rather, a lot depends on whether other powerful states (especially the existing hegemon) attempt to suppress it, hence creating its dissatisfaction with the system, in the sense used by Jacek Kugler above. This

[26] *Current History*, vol. 105, no. 690 (April 2006): 160–62.

subtle change almost reverses Mearsheimer's own views aired in his 2000 *Foreign Affairs* article. But, one thing is sure. The Mearsheimer of 2006 is more in keeping with a growing trend in the intellectual climate on the China debate in America.

China's Power Deficit

There is a very different approach to assessing, nay, demystifying, the "China threat" by comparing the nitty-gritty of power between China and the United States, across the whole spectrum of military power, alliance networks, diplomatic savvyness, soft power, and even economic strength.[27] In this esoteric literature, China loses on almost all scores. It is obvious that China cannot match the United States in military might, alliance networks, or diplomacy. What is less obvious, but no less significant, is that China is found to have a "soft power deficit."[28] The analyst who drew this conclusion was Joseph S. Nye, who was the first one to develop the concept of "soft power" to mean a country's ability to influence others to what it wants without force or coercion.[29]

On the economic front, too, China may not necessarily be ahead in the longer term. If assuming overall Chinese GDP passes that of the United States around 2030, Nye points out, "the two economies would be equivalent in size but not equal in composition." There will still be a vast underdeveloped countryside, and it will then face "demographic problems from the delayed effects of the one-child per couple policy it enforced in the 20th century."[30] His calculation factors

---

[27] For example, Joseph S. Nye, Jr., *The Future of Power* (New York: Public Affairs, 2011); David Shambaugh, *China Goes Global: The Partial Power* (Oxford University Press, 2013); Thomas Christensen, *The China Challenge: Shaping the Choice of a Rising Power* (New York: W.W. Norton, 2015); Lionel Vairion, *China Threat: The Challenges, and Realities of China's Rise* (New York: CN Times Books, 2013), and so on.

[28] Joseph S. Nye, Jr., "China's Soft Power Deficit," *Wall Street Journal*, May 8, 2012.

[29] Joseph S. Nye, Jr., *Soft Power: The Means to Success in World Politics* (New York: Public Affairs, 2014).

[30] Joseph S. Nye, Jr., *The Future of Power*, see note 27, at 180.

in the natural tendency that growth of an emerging economy will slow after reaching a developed stage. So, even assuming the Chinese growth rate can be maintained at 6% annually, to America's 2%, after 2030, "China would not equal the United States in per capita income until sometime in the second half of the century . . ."[31]

Shifts in the China Debate and Trump's Attitudinal Shifts

As we have noticed in Chapter 6, Trump the President has mellowed since inauguration from Trump the candidate during the 2016 campaign. One particular example we noted was in his change of opinion, after he took office, on his earlier condemnation of China as a currency manipulator. Besides, keen observers may have noticed a discernible decline in the bellicosity of President Trump's rhetoric and attitude about China. This shift is most obvious in his own comments hailing "tremendous" progress after his Mar-a-Lago tete-a-tete with President Xi Jinping of China, on April 6–7, 2017. Nevertheless, the euphoria was followed shortly thereafter by some flip-flops that came in rapid succession, following Trump's tweeted complaint about China not trying hard enough to reign in the nuclear ambitious North Koreans. He angered the Chinese by approving a $1.4 billion arms sales to Taiwan on June 28 and by allowing the warship Stethem to cruise within the 12-mile territorial waters of the Triton Island, in the Paracel island group claimed by China in the SCS, which took place on July 2. In addition, the Trump Administration imposed sanctions on a Chinese bank it accused as a conduit for illicit North Korean financial activity. White House also announced it would act against imported Chinese steel. But, true to his unpredictable reputation, Trump made a phone call, on July 3, to President Xi, to appeal for more help to restrain what he called the "growing threat" posed by North Korea. White House took Xi's willingness to take the call in very positive light.[32]

---

[31] Ibid.

[32] "After Angering China, Trump Talks with its Leader about North Korea," *New York Times*, July 3, 2017, online.

While the media may be left puzzling about this latest telephone exchange between the two leaders, which came in the wake of Trump's flip-flops just noted, I tend to view this latest development differently. I really think that after the procession of the shifts in the intellectual climate in the "China threat" debate, as just noted, the final message that came crystal clear to President Trump, after his first 100 days in office, is that in a world of "vulnerability interdependence" (in Rosecrance's terms), a hegemonic war between the United States and China would be suicidal for both of them. Besides, the nuclear ambitious North Korea poses a threat to both superpowers, albeit to different degrees. It would be wise for the United States to keep China on its side in a concerted effort to cope with North Korea, in a way reminiscent of the Nixon–Kissingerian scenario of making China a partner in the joint enterprise of constraining the heftily nuclear-armed Soviet Union in the 1970s.

Furthermore, I am willing to argue, two related effects, in particular, that may have been rubbed off on the Trump administration from the deepening China-threat debate, noted above, were (a) that power alone does not necessarily make an ascending China expansive, and (b) what makes a difference is whether China has the "intention" to upset the existing globalized world order. Thus, unlike the Obama administration, the Trump administration seems more attuned to ascertaining China's sensibilities, including its receptiveness to U.S. concerns about a rogue state like North Korea. This is why after Trump's July 3 call, the White House was so pleased that Xi took the call with no qualms, which was viewed as an indication that "he was not ready to escalate tensions with the United States"[33] despite the flip-flops on the part of Trump noted earlier.

China's Scofflaw Stigma Over SCS and Its Exoneration

Now that the China-threat scare seems to have lost much of its earlier punch, as has been shown in the increasing dissatisfaction, among a wide circle of commentators, with the earlier realist alarmist

[33] Ibid.

assessments, the next remaining hurdle confronting China, if it is concerned with its good name in the international community, is its scofflaw stigma, the origin of which we discussed in Chapter 4.

At the time of this writing, the gap between Europe (as well as much of the rest of the world) and President Trump's America seems to be widening, on account of his defiance of the world's consensus on the global climate and, moreover, his rejection of globalized free trade in favor of protectionism, accruing from his "America First" campaign slogan. A growing sense seems to be emerging that, in the words of two coauthors writing in the *Foreign Affairs*, "the future of globalization will depend on China."[34] This same dissatisfaction with Trump that led commentators to turn toward China's Xi Jinping as an alternative leader was echoed by Angela Stanzel, at the European Council on Foreign Relations in Berlin, when she remarked: "The election of Trump has facilitated China's aims in Europe," adding: "Trump facilitates China's narrative of being the defender of multilateralism and especially global free trade,. . . and it fits into the Chinese idea of creating an alternative leadership to the United States."[35]

In Chapter 7, we have noted that China under Xi Jinping deliberately chose a geo-economics-oriented strategy in order to pursue a course of "nonsymmetric" competition with the United States. Its ultimate purpose was specifically to veer off from a geopolitical conflict, away from competing with the United States for global leadership. The subsequent suggestions to the contrary by commentators as geographically wide apart as the coauthors of the *Foreign Affairs* article (Fred Hu and Michael Spence) in America and Angela Stanzel in Germany came as an extraneous, certainly unanticipated, outcome from Xi's original choice of his geo-economic strategy. Hence, China finds itself forced into a leadership position by default, as a result of U.S. retreat on the named fronts under the Trump presidency. But, if it is going to ready itself for this by-default leadership role, China must

[34] Fred Hu and Michael Spence, "Why Globalization Stalled," *Foreign Affairs*, vol. 96, no, 4 (July/August 2017), 141–48, 142.

[35] Quoted in "As Europe Backs Away from U.S. Position, China Quietly Steps into Breach," *New York Times*, July 6, 2017, 9, column 1.

ultimately establish its credentials as a clean, respectable, "authority" (in the sense David Lake used it above)[36] with an inspiring moral rectitude and unequivocal commitment to a rules-based world order. In this light, China must do everything within its power to rid itself of the scofflaw stigma that it has brought upon itself by its repudiation of the PCA arbitral tribunal's award that finds China at fault, as its SCS claims are summarily denied validity under the UNCLOS III. Since the PCA tribunal's award is not subject to appeal, China must perforce seek vindication of its innocence through an adjudicative procedure allowable under the terms of the same treaty under which it lost the arbitral case in the China–Philippines case, as discussed in Chapter 4.

Let us recall that the case was brought by the Philippines to the PCA arbitration procedures under Annex 7 of UNCLOS III. And, according to Article 11 of the same Annex 7, on the "Finality of Award," it is clearly stated that "the award shall be final and without appeal." However, Article 12 provides for a procedure which may serve to offer what in effect amounts to an "appeal" opportunity, though without the name. Article 12 is on the modality of resolving a controversy regarding interpretation or implementation if a controversy should occur. In the Philippine–China case, the controversy is about the interpretation of the final award in which the tribunal relied on the provisions of UNCLOS III, to the exclusion of general (customary) international law. Art. 12 (2) provides: "Any such controversy may be submitted to another court or tribunal under Article 287 (of UNCLOS III) by agreement of all the parties to the dispute." And, Art. 287 of the Convention offers a choice of four such forums:

1. The ITLOS (International Tribunal for Law of the Sea), established inaccordance with Annex VI of the Convention
2. The International Court of Justice (ICJ)
3. An arbitral tribunal constituted in accordance with Annex VII
4. A special arbitral tribunal constituted in accordance with Annex XII

[36] David Lake, see note 14.

Besides, and more important, the preamble of the UNCLOS III proclaims that "matters not regulated by this Convention continue to be governed by the rules and principles of general international law." Since the tribunal in the arbitration between the Philippines and China did not follow this injunction, but arrived at its rulings totally in disregard of the "rules and principles of general international law," on the matter of historic waters, which is the legal basis of the Chinese claim to the SCS maritime region. China, therefore, has a right to seek an "interpretation" from one of the above four forums, as to why this injunction was ignored by the Arbitral Tribunal, as much as "historic waters" is a matter not regulated by CLOS III; and, hence, the legitimacy of the tribunal's final award is in doubt, as it was reached without regard to the preamble's injunction.

In its request for an interpretation as such, China has the opportunity to restructure the questions to be addressed from the standpoint of general international law, to break away from the trap set by the unilateral discretion of the Philippines, via its *compromis d'arbitrage* — which asked the Tribunal to examine the case against the provisions of UNCLOS III alone — as a result of the nonparticipation of China.

In the event, however, that the Philippines should refuse to sign off on an agreement required by Art. 12 (2) of Annex VII, if a request for interpretation is to proceed, then China may take the initiative of filing an independent suit before the ICJ against the Arbitral Tribunal that heard the Philippines–China case. The ground of the charge in the suit would be the tribunal's blatant failure to treat the case as one concerning "historic waters," thus arriving at its negative conclusions in total disregard of general international law, as the UNCCLOS III contains nothing in its entirety on the issue of historic waters.

An Equitable Restructuring of the Issues at Stake

If and when China should come before the ICJ, either in a joint (with the Philippines) request for an interpretation or in an independent suit, to seek a redress of injustice, the issues to be heard by the Court would be stacked up very differently. Two cardinal questions for the attention of the Court would begin with: (a) the historic waters versus the territorial waters and exclusive economic zone (EEZs) in the SCS. To assess this question, an answer must be sought from another question, namely: (b) sovereignty over the four major island groups in the SCS. Ultimately, historic waters and the sovereignty issue (i.e., who owns the four island groups) hold the key to all disputed issues.

Logical Conclusions Under General International Law: End of Disputes

In this hypothetical adjudication, when the ICJ proceeds with the issues of historic waters and sovereignty foremost in mind and applies general international law, its reasoning would follow five steps, in reaching a final decision capable of ending all the disputes regarding the SCS.

1. In the first step, the Court would address the cardinal question of who owns the four major island groups in the SCS, the Paracels, Spratlys, Pratas, and Ecclesfield Bank. Looking seriously into the facts of history, the Court would find China wields unchallengeable sovereignty over these Island groups, both by historicity (China's control and jurisdiction going back to the 3rd century BC until modern times) and in light of their return at the end of World War II by Japan, whose Imperial Army had briefly occupied these islands from the 1930s on until 1945 — their return, required by the Cairo (1943) and Potsdam (1945) Declarations, was acknowledged expressly in the Instrument of Surrender Japan signed on September 2, 1945, on the USS Missouri.
2. The next step would be to establish that the spread of the four major island groups, in reality, has the effect of a configuration of an archipelagic extension of the Chinese land mass.
3. A logical following step from the above would be to determine the legal status of two bodies of water, viz.: (a) the waters between the islands, islets, and atolls within the four major island groups; and (b) the waters surrounding the four Island groups.

To use a common denominator, the two bodies of water combine to form the "historic waters" of China, which has sovereignty over the archipelagic constellation of the four major Island groups, and all features within them, in the SCS, as cartographically encircled by the nine-dash line.

4. The next step would be to ascertain the legal status of the U-shaped nine-dash line, beginning with the year (1947) when the map was drawn and publicly promulgated, as is noted in Chapter 2. To the extent the drawing of the line did not deviate from the principle of characterizing the two bodies of water above, it conforms to what is allowable under general international law. The Line which circumscribes the historic waters of China, besides, conformed to the contemporaneous international law (of 1947), as attested to by the absence of objection by any country or territory (including colonies) at the time.
5. The final step, drawing everything to a concluding decision, would be to affirm the finding that (a) the nine-dash line encloses the Chinese historic waters, (b) due to China's sovereignty over the four major island groups in the SCS, all the islands, islets, atolls, and other features located therein combine to form China's archipelagic extension; and (c) the body of China's historic waters, therefore, delineates the extent of the maritime region encircled by the Line. Other States enjoy only the right of navigation (RON) in these Chinese historic waters, and nothing else.

The Court could hand down this decision either as a response to a presumptive joint request for an "interpretation" of the PCA Arbitration Tribunal's 2016 Final Award (in the PIs-China arbitration case) or as a judgment in China's suit against the same Tribunal. In that event, all territorial disputes would be resolved, because all other competing claims would be invalidated, once the historic waters issue is thus settled in China's favor. In addition, it would in effect nullify the final award by the PCA Arbitral Tribunal in the Philippines–China case. Thereby, China's scofflaw stigma would be fully exonerated.

Conclusion

A decision thus rendered by the ICJ would not only settle, once for all, all legal disputes arising from the overlapping claims by the competing claimants. But, it would also deprive any ex-regional power, like the United States, of an ax to grind, such as claiming a nonrestrictive FON as a shield for its targeted naval surveillance activities. Once China's historic-waters claim is substantiated under general international law (as opposed to treaty law), by a decision of the authoritative ICJ, then the status of the waters between the U-shaped nine-dash line and the coastlines of the surrounding coastal states — Vietnam, Malaysia, Brunei, and the Philippines — is different from the waters found within the encirclement of the U-shaped line. The former body of waters, depending on its width, may consist of parts of the high seas beyond the territorial seas and EEZs of the coastal states. The latter body of waters includes the territorial seas and EEZs of the China-owned island groups, and waters that are analogous to the territorial sea in its legal status. In this latter maritime region, foreign ships (U.S. ships included) have the right of "innocent passage" only, under modern law of the sea. Any passage aimed at naval surveillance, harassment, or intimidation is, obviously, not "innocent."

When the smoldering SCS disputes are thus resolved once for all through this adjudicative mode, and when there is no room for naval surveillance or activities by foreign warships to challenge China's rights in SCS based on historicity, thus ending the U.S.–China contest, chances are that it will be the beginning of peace, in and out of the SCS. And, with the China-threat scare receding to the background, and the removal of China's scofflaw stigma via the same adjudicative process, the United States will find it possible to meet China across the SCS divide. Together, they may find it possible to establish a condominium as the copreservers of world peace and order, on an equal footing. It will be a new world order in a new era under a new condominium.

Amen.

References

Abramowitz, Morton, and Stephen Bosworth. 2006 April. "American Confronts the Asian Century." *Current History* 105 (690):147.

Adler, Mortimer J., ed. 1976. *The Revolutionary Years. Britannica's Book of the American Revolution*. Chicago: Encyclopedia Britannica.

Allison, Graham. 2017. *Destined for War: Can America and China Escape Thucydides Trap?* Boston: Houghton Mifflin Harcourt.

Beard, Charles. 1966. *The Idea of National Interest, an Analytical Study of American Foreign Policy*. Chicago: Quadrangle Books.

Bouchez, Leo J. 1964. *The Regime of Bays in International Law*. The Hague: Martinus Nijhoff.

Brown, Peter. 2009. "Calculated Ambiguity in the South China Sea." *Asia Times*, December 8.

Buszynski, Leszek. 2012. "The South China Sea: Oil, Maritime Claims, and U.S.–China Strategic Rivalry." *The Washington Quarterly* 35 (Spring):139–56.

Chan, Steve. 2012. *Looking for Balance: China and the U.S., and Power Balancing in East Asia*. Stanford: Stanford University Press.

Chang, Te-Kuang. 1991. "China's Claim of Sovereignty over Spratly and Paracel Islands: A Historical and Legal Perspective." *Case Western Reserve Journal of International Law* 23 (3):399–420.

Ching, Frank. 1994. "Paracels Islands Dispute." *Far Eastern Economic Review, February 10, 1994.* (*The China Challenge: Shaping the Choice of a Rising Power*).

Cohen, Jerome A., and Hungdah Chiu, eds. 1974. *People's China and International Law*. New Jersey: Princeton University Press, 2 vols.

Coolidge, Mary Roberts. 1968. *Chinese Immigration*. New York: Holt, 1909; reprinted by the Ch'eng-wen Publishing.

Denlinger, Paul. 2016. "Will China Do Something to Defend Their Position about the South China Sea Controversy?" *Quora*, July 16. http://www.linkedin/pauldenlinger.

Dorwart, Jeffrey M. 1975. *The Pigtail War: America in the Sino-JapaneseWar of 1894–1895.* Massachusetts: University of Massachusetts Press.

Dreyer, Edward I. 2007. *Zheng He: China and the Oceans in the Early Ming Dynasty, 1405–1433.* New York: Pearson/Longman.

Dupuy, Forian, and Pierre-Marie Dupuy. 2013 January. "A Legal Analysis of China's Historic Rights Claim in the South China Sea." *American Journal of International Law* 107 (1):124–41.

Dzurek, Daniel J. 1985. "Boundary and Resources Disputes in the South China Sea." In *Ocean Yearbook 5*, edited by E. Mann Borgese, E., and N. Ginsburg, 254–84. Chicago: University of Chicago Press.

Fairbank, John K., ed. 1968. *The Chinese World Order: Traditional Chinese Foreign Relations.* Cambridge: Harvard University Press.

Firestein, David. 2016. "The U.S.–China Perception Gap in the South China Sea." *The Diplomat,* August 19.

Frank, Andre Gunder. 1998. *ReOrient: Global Economy in the Asian Age.* Berkley: University of California Press.

Fu, Kuen-Chen. 1995. *Nan (zhongguo) hai falv diwei zhi yanjiu* (*Legal Status of the South (China) Sea*). Taipei: 123 Publications.

Garver, John. 2006. *China and Iran: Ancient Partners in the Post-Imperial World.* Seattle: University of Washington Press.

Glaser, John. 2017. "Tillerson's South China Sea Proposal Won't Work," *The Diplomat,* January 14.

Gordner, Lee G. 1994. "The Spratly Islands Dispute and the Law of the Sea." *Ocean Development and International Law* 25 (1):61–74.

Gordon, Philip. 2017 March–April. "A Vision of Tump at War: How the President Could Stumble into Conflict." *Foreign Affairs* 96 (3).

Green, Michael J. 2017. *By More Than Providence: Grand Strategy and American Power in the Asia Pacific Since 1783.* New York: Columbia University Press.

Gulick, Edward Vose. 1973. *Peter Parker and the Opening of China.* Cambridge: Harvard University Press.

Gupta, Sourabh. 2017. "Alternative Facts and the Threat in the South China Sea." *East Asia Forum,* February 14.

———. 2014. *PacNet #88 — Testing China's — and State Department's Nine-Dash Line Claims.* Washington, DC: Center for Strategic and International Studies.

Han, Jen-hua, ed. 1985. *A Compilation of Historic Documents and Materials Relating to South China Sea Islands.* Beijing: Dongfang Publishers, 172–79.

Hayton, Bill. 2014. *The South China Sea: The Struggle for Power in Asia.* New Haven: Yale University Press.

Hertslet, Edward. 1908. *Treaties, etc., between China and Foreign Powers.*

Houn, Franklin W. 1973. *A Short History of Chinese Communism.* Englewood Cliffs: Prentice Hall.

Hu, Fred, and Michael Spence. 2017 July/August. "Why Globalization Stalled?" *Foreign Affairs* 96 (4):141–48.

Hsiung, James. 1997. *Anarchy and Order: The Interplay of Politics and Law in International Relations.* Boulder: Lynne Rienner.

———. 2012. *China into Its Second Rise. Myths, Puzzles, Paradoxes, and Challenge to Theory.* Singapore: World Scientific.

———. 2015. "Utility vs. Inadequacy of Realist Theory: Assessing China's Rise," *International Studies Review* 17 (1):132–37.

———. 2016. "Nanhai zhi zheng: guojifa yu zhongguo ruhe huwei ziji quanyi [The Disputes over the South China Sea: International Law and How China Can Defend Its Own Rights]." In *Zhongguo pinglun* (China Review) (Hong Kong) (February), 43–45.

Hsiung, James, and Steven I. Levine, eds. 1992. *China's Bitter Victory: The War with Japan, 1937–1945.* Armonk: M. E. Sharpe.

Hsiung, James, and Winberg Chai, eds. 1981. *Asia and U.S. Foreign Policy.* New York: Praeger.

Hunt, Michael H. 1973. *Frontier Defense and the Open Door: Manchuria in Chinese American Relations, 1895–1911.* New Haven: Yale University Press.

Jacques, Martin. 2009. *When China Rules the World: The End of the West and the Birth of a New Global Order.* New York: The Penguin Press.

Jones, Eric. 1988. *Growth Recurring, Economic Change in World History.* Oxford: Clarendon Press.

Kang, David. 2010. *East Asia before the West: Five Centuries of Trade and Tribute*. New York: Columbia University Press.

Kaplan, Robet D. 2015. *Asia's Cauldron: The South China Sea and the End of a Stable Pacific*. New York: Random House.

Kausikan, Bilahari. 2017. "Asia in the Trump Era: From Pivot to Peril?" *Foreign Affairs* 96 (3).

Kenny, Henry J. 2002. *Shadow of the Dragon: Vietnam's Struggle with China and the Implications for the U.S. Foreign Policy*, 61–64. Washington, DC: Potomac Books.

Kissinger, Henry. 2011. *On China*. New York: The Penguin Press.

Kugler, Jacek. 2006. "The Asian Ascent: Opportunity for Peace or Precondition for War?" *International Studies Perspective*. 7 (1):36–42.

Lake, David. 2003. "The New Sovereignty in International Relations," *International Studies Review* 4 (5):303–23.

Lo, Chi-kin. 2004. *China's Policy towards Territorial Disputes: The Case of the South China Sea Islands*. London: Taylor & Francis.

Lu, Ning. 1993. *The Spratly Archipelago: The Origins of the Claims and Possible Solutions*. Washington, DC: International Center.

Maddison, Angus. 2007. *Contours of the World Economy: 1-2030 A.D.* Oxford: University of Oxford Press.

———. 2003. *The World Economy: Historical Statistics*. Paris: OECD.

Mearsheimer, John F. 2006 April. "China's Unpeaceful Rise." *Current History* 105 (690):160–62.

———. 2001. "The Future of the American Pacifier." *Foreign Affairs* (September–October), 46–61.

Mitter, Rana. 1992. *The Forgotten Ally: China's World War II, 1937–1945* Cambridge: Houghton Mifflin Harcourt.

Morse, Hosa Ballou. 1910. *The International Relations of the Chinese Empire: The Period of Conflict, 1834–1860*. London: Longmans, Greens.

Nye, Joseph, Jr. 2011. *The Future of Power*. New York: Public Affairs.

Park, Coon-ho. 1978. "The South China Sea Disputes: Who Owns the Islands and the Natural Resources." *Ocean Development and International Law Journal* 5 (1):33ff.

Pharandm D., and Y. Keabza. 1993. *The Continental Shelf and Economic Zone: Delimitation of Legal Regime*. Kluwer.

Pratt, Julius W. 1964. *Expansionists of 1898, the Acquisition of Hawaii and the Spanish Islands*. Chicago: Quadrangle Books.

———. 1972. *A History of U.S. Foreign Policy*. Englewood Cliffs: Prentice-Hall.

Pye, Lucian W. 1991. *China, an Introduction.* 4th ed. New York: HarperCollins.

Rosecrance, Richard. 1972. *The Future of the International Strategic System.* San Francisco: Chandler.

———. 2006. "Power and International Relations: The Rise of China And Its Effects," *International Studies Perspectives* 7 (1):31–35.

Scott, David. 2008. *China and the International System, 1840–1949: Power, Presence, and Perceptions in a Century of Humiliation.* Albany: SUNY Press.

Scott, Edward. 1908. *Treaties, etc., between China and Foreign Powers.* London: Harrison & Sons.

Shao, Hsun-cheng. 1956. "Chinese Islands in the South China Sea." Translated by Jerome Cohen and Hungdah Chiu (1974), Vol. I: 344–45.

Shirk, Susan. 2017. "Trump and China." *Foreign Affairs* 96 (2):20–27.

Song, Yann-huei, and Peter Kien-hong Yu. 1994. "China's 'Historic Waters' in the South China Sea: An Analysis from Taiwan, Republic of China." *American Asian Review* (New York) 12 (4):89–101.

Spykman, Nicolas John. 1944. *Geography of the Peace.* New York: Harcourt, Brace.

Symmons, Clive R. 2008. *Historic Waters in the Law of the Sea: A Modern Re-Appraisal.* The Hague: Martinus Nijhoff.

Tammen, Roland L., Jacek Kugler, Douglas Lemke, Carole Alsharabati, Brian Efird, A. F. K. Organski. 2000. *Power Transitions: Strategies for the 21st Century.* New York: Seven Bridges Press.

Taylor, Tim. 2012. "The Rights Stuff in Oil Islands Row." *The Lawyer,* October 15.

Tong, Te-Kong. 1977. "The Manchus and the Yankees, 1784–1911." Paper presented at the Asian-American Assembly for Policy Research, City College of New York, CUNY, April 29.

———. 1964. *United States Diplomacy in China, 1844–1860.* Seattle: University of Washington Press.

Tung, William L. 1970. *China and the Foreign Powers.* Dobbs Ferry: Oceana Publications.

U.N. International Law Commission. 1962. "Judicial Regime of Historic Waters Including Historic Bays — Study Prepared by the Secretariat," Document A/Cn.4/145, *Yearbook of the U.N. International Law Commission.*

U.S. Department of State, Bureau of Oceans. 1992. *Limits in the Sea, No. 114: U.S. Responses to Excessive Maritime Claims* (March 9).11

Van Dyke, Jon M., and Dale L. Bennett. 1993. "Islands and the Delimitation of Ocean Space in the South China Sea." *Ocean Yearbook* 10:54–89.

Valencia, Mark, Jon M. Van Dyke, and Noel A. Ludwig. 1999. *Sharing the Resources of the South China Sea*. Paperback ed. Honolulu: University of Hawaii Press.

Van Ness, Peter. 2002. "Hegemony, Not Anarchy: Why China and Japan Are Not Balancing Against U.S., Unipolar Power," *International Relations of the Asia Pacific* (Tokyo) 2 (1):131–50.

Waltz, Kenneth N. 1979. *Theory of International Politics.* Reading: Addison-Wesley Publishing.

________. 2000. "Structural Realism after the Cold War." *International Security* 25 (1):5–41.

Weber, Katja. 2000. *Hierarchy amidst Anarchy.* Albany: State University Press.

White, Hugh. 2017. "China's Belt and Road Initiative to Challenge U.S.-Led Order." *East Asian Forum*, May 8.

Yeh, S. 1988. "Nansha fengyun he guoji gongfa [The Nansha Imbroglio and International Law]", cited in Te-kuang Chang 1991.

Zhirinejad, Mahnaz. 2010. "Implication of New World Order on China's Energy Policy towards Iran." *Asia-Pacific Journal of Social Sciences* Special Issue No. 1 (December).

Index